HOW TO MASTER PERSONALITY QUESTIONNAIRES

SECOND EDITION

MARK PARKINSON

**KOGAN
PAGE**

'A round man cannot be expected to fit in a square hole right away. He must have time to modify his shape.'

Mark Twain

First published in 1997
Second edition 2000

Kogan Page Limited
120 Pentonville Road
London N1 9JN
UK

Kogan Page US
163 Central Avenue, Suite 2
Dover NH 03820
USA

© Mark Parkinson, 1997, 2000

British Library Cataloguing in Publication Data

A CIP record for this book is available from the British Library

ISBN 0 7494 3419 8

Typeset by Jean Cussons Typesetting, Diss, Norfolk
Printed and bound in Great Britain by Clays Ltd, St

Contents

To the Reader

As a psychologist, I am frequently asked what personality questionnaires are, how they work, and how they should be completed. In fact, some days my telephone runs hot with employers asking about the different way of measuring people's personality and with potential test candidates wanting advice on the assessment process. Others just want to know more about how they can understand their own personality better, so that they can take charge of their own development, and improve their career prospects.

This book is based on the advice I give to people who contact me, and also on the various talks I have given over the years. My intention is to give you some essential inside information and, more importantly, some practical help.

All the information in this book is in the public domain. However, much of it is technical or difficult to find. I have simply done what you could do if you had the time and knew where to look. I also believe that it is important to demystify psychological testing, and to demonstrate the benefits and pitfalls to employer and test-taker alike. After all, the cloaking of testing in complete secrecy and the belief that psychologists are only one step removed from alchemists, does no one any good at all.

The results of my endeavours are presented in a way that I

hope you will find entertaining and informative. As this is the second edition of this book, I have included details on some of the latest developments in personality measurement, in particular 'emotional intelligence', and a description of the most popular questionnaire used in career development: the Myers-Briggs Type Indicator™.

Readers have also said that they would like to see an extract from the narrative report for the Occupational Personality Questionnaire (OPQ®), so I have included this at the end of the book. The OPQ is now the UK's leading personality questionnaire and is used for both selection and development purposes. Finally, do not forget that Chapter 5 contains a specially written questionnaire, the Mind Style Questionnaire, for you to try.

Mark Parkinson
Berkshire 2000

Introduction

The last 20 years have seen a steady increase in the use of all types of psychological tests. Nowadays, if you go for a job with a medium- to large-sized organisation, you stand about a 75 per cent chance of being tested. The tests are used at all levels, from clerical and production positions to managerial and professional staff.

The subject of this book is the personality test, or, strictly speaking, the personality questionnaire. To clarify any misunderstanding, while the word 'test' is widely used, it gives the impression that questions about personality have right or wrong answers. This is not the case as no one type of personality, in itself, is necessarily 'better' than any other. The element of selection comes in comparing people's differing personalities with the requirements for a job.

Personality questionnaires are big business – for example, the most popular questionnaire is used to assess about 3.5 million people per year. This is on a global basis, of course, but the figure is still very impressive. One of the main reasons for the increase is the shift towards service or people-orientated industries – hence the importance of assessing the type of working relationships that people prefer, both with colleagues and customers. Another reason is that questionnaires can provide reliable information not only quickly but cheaply as well, because many people can be assessed at the same time. Well-constructed questionnaires are also a fairer way of assessing personality as most interviewers are unskilled in this area.

The use of personality questionnaires is not without criticism. Many people object to being categorised and maintain it is impossible to measure something as complicated as personality. This is an understandable argument but it slightly misses the point. It is true that our personalities are complex, but there are obvious similarities and differences between people, and this is what questionnaires highlight. It is these broad and enduring factors that are used to help in the job selection process.

Another major objection to questionnaires is that people behave differently in different situations. Again, this is perfectly true, but whether or not you find yourself in a particular situation presumably has something to do with your personality. What personality questionnaires are doing is predicting what you are most likely to do. This does not mean that you always do the same thing, rather that, given a particular set of circumstances, you are more likely than not to behave in a certain manner. This should make sense, as we know from personal experience that people do not react to things in a completely random way.

Finally, people believe that the use of questionnaires is in some way underhand and that employers and psychologists have bad intentions. Indeed, a recent magazine article made much of the expression 'personality inventory': ' "Inventory" is sometimes used as a synonym for "questionnaire" or "test" '. The thrust of the piece was that the expression 'personality inventory' conjures up a picture of someone making a list of assets or attempting to detail all the positive qualities of a person. But what about the negative aspects? Surely personality questionnaires are measuring both the positive *and* the negative qualities, argued the author. Yet again, this is true, but somewhat off-target. Any sort of personality assessment does cover both sides of the equation, but a particular personality is neither 'good' nor 'bad', 'positive' nor 'negative'. Whether or not your personality fits a specific work setting depends entirely on what you are trying to do.

So what are employers looking for? This question will be considered in much more detail later on, but basically as employers can be far more choosy nowadays, they can also be more precise about the personality characteristics they demand of their employees.

For many jobs, qualities such as self-reliance, flexibility, the ability to plan ahead, and to work as part of a team are important. For managerial positions, the emphasis can shift to leadership, drive, problem solving and the ability to motivate others; sales people, on the other hand, require persuasiveness, adaptability, resilience and confidence. All of these aspects of personality are of key importance in one way or another. So, for example, an inflexible and domineering manager is unlikely to be particularly successful; likewise, a shy and hesitant salesman is unlikely to progress.

As an applicant for a job, it is obviously useful to know what an employer is searching for and how he or she will assess you. In addition, you should bear in mind that you will not only come across personality questionnaires through job hunting as part of the selection process, but when you are in a job as well. Personality questionnaires are routinely used for assessing and developing people *during* employment. An additional use is for careers guidance or personal counselling.

About this book

To help you to understand personality questionnaires, this book explains:

- The origins and nature of personality.
- The thinking behind personality questionnaires.

- The different types of personality questionnaires.
- What employers do with questionnaire results.
- How to identify and change your behaviour.
- The major questionnaires in use today.

It also includes a working personality questionnaire. This is designed using the latest thinking on personality measurement, and will give you a useful assessment of your own personality and valuable 'test' practice.

To conclude, it may be that you resent the idea of somebody probing your personality. It may be that you think it cannot actually be done. However, like it or not, it is an increasingly common practice, and the fact is that you will miss many employment opportunities if you don't take part in personality assessments. This book is about giving you the best possible chance of getting the job you want, and alerting you to some of the tricks of the psychologist's trade.

Note: Masculine pronouns are used in this book to avoid awkward grammatical constructions. In most instances, feminine pronouns can be used interchangeably.

1

What is Personality?

There are about 20,000 words in the English language that describe personality. Every day we use them when we talk about other people. We say that someone is like this or that, that someone else has 'lots of personality', or 'no personality' at all. In fact, sometimes we just use the word personality by itself, as in 'TV personality'. What we are actually doing is describing either particular personality characteristics or in some way, quantity of personality.

The idea that we have different quantities of personality is interesting, if a little misleading. It is more accurate to say that we all have different patterns of personality and so differ in all sorts of complex ways, than to argue about amounts. Also, when it comes to quantity we are frequently referring to social success or public 'attractiveness'. Interestingly, these aspects of an individual are far more likely to be the *consequence* of a particular personality than something already built into that person.

Furthermore, the words we use encapsulate a particular sort of behaviour and these can also describe how we would expect that person to react. For example, if I tell you that someone is very shy, you would not expect him or her to earn a living selling products or to like large social gatherings. So the words we use label a characteristic pattern of behaviour because it is true of a number of different situations; the description also provides a clue about how someone might think or feel. This leads us to consider personality as being stable because it does not change dramatically over time. For instance, when you wake up each morning, you are *always* the same sort of person.

You may wake up in a different mood from the previous morning, but your basic personality will not have changed radically overnight. However, the idea that personality and behaviour are the same thing is not correct. They certainly are not the same because if they were you would always react in completely predictable ways.

In reality, personality is best thought of as moderating your behaviour, or as guiding it in particular directions. This allows you to react in a number of ways that are natural to you, depending on the circumstances. So, if you are looking for a definition, personality is the characteristic way in which someone responds to situations, or, if you like, their preferred way of behaving towards particular circumstances and other people.

To summarise, the important features of personality are that:

- It stems from you as an individual.
- It predicts your behaviour over a range of situations.
- It doesn't alter dramatically over time.
- It distinguishes you in meaningful ways from other people.

However, to complicate matters further, personality is also influenced by your beliefs, which you hold to be true despite the fact that there may be no evidence for them; and by your values, which are really the set of beliefs against which you judge your own and other people's behaviour. You could also add motivation, or the aspect of your character that drives your behaviour: why you do what you do. This is usually expressed in terms of needs, such as the need to be successful or to be secure. Clearly, all these factors also have a part to play in explaining personality.

Where does personality come from?

There are at least three answers to this question. Some psychologists maintain that personality is a matter of genetics, while others argue that it is a question of how you were brought up and of life experience. Many believe that it is a combination of both factors. Whatever the answer, as a well-known wit said, make sure you choose your parents with care!

If we examine these ideas more closely, there are aspects of our behaviour that do appear to be automatic. This leads us to describe certain actions as being 'due to human nature', the implication being that some behavioural patterns are automatic functions of our brains. However, unlike the reactions of many other animals, this instinctual behaviour is not very strong. For example, while many women have a maternal instinct, it is not true of all women. If it were, we would be able to predict *exactly* a whole range of female behaviour. We cannot because the same stimulus does not produce the same reaction in everyone. This means that people are very unlikely by nature to be inherently maternal, outgoing, criminal, or whatever.

Alongside the 'human nature' view of behaviour, we often stereotype people on the basis of their body build. Characteristically, we think of large, round people as being full of life and jolly, and tall, thin people as introspective and gloomy. Indeed, in the 1950s a psychologist called Sheldon classified people into three types according to their build:

- **Endomorphs.** These are well-rounded, usually slightly overweight people who like eating, drinking and socialising. They are drawn to other people.
- **Ectomorphs.** These are thin, delicate people who are sensitive and prone to worrying. They don't like social gatherings and can appear cold.
- **Mesomorphs.** These are muscular, well-built and energetic people who are very direct in their approach to things. They can sometimes be rather insensitive.

Again, this is a generic argument for personality. However, despite its attractiveness, it should come as no surprise that there is little evidence for any link between the way in which your body is constructed and your personality. This is no doubt a disappointment to novelists who have frequently used body size as an indicator of character. A well-known example is a description by HG Wells in *The Truth about Pyecraft*: 'He behaved exactly as I should expect a great, fat fellow to behave – badly'. Yet in saying this, with regard to the particular case of the relationship between body size and sociability, there may be a factor at work. It is more subtle than simply classifying someone into one of three broad categories. Thus, if large people are expected to be outgoing and bubbly, this may be encouraged by others over time, so that they actually start to act in the expected manner. In this way, being sociable is reinforced and the whole idea becomes self-fulfilling.

Nowadays most psychologists believe that personality may have some genetic component, but that it must also be influenced by how you were brought up and the sorts of experiences you have had throughout your life. Interestingly, while many people may disagree with the content of this theory, this was broadly the view taken by the most famous personality theorist of them all – Sigmund Freud. His psychoanalytic theory is not easy to summarise in a few words, but essentially he argued that our personalities are formed early in life, especially as a result of our experiences during the first five years, and that we are driven by a need for pleasure. Although the theory is very extensive – Freud's collected works run to some 24 volumes – it is, unfortunately, untestable.

Psychoanalysis apart, modern personality theory usually boils down to one of two varieties: trait or type. The approaches rely on different underlying principles, but both are attempts to simplify the behaviour associated with particular personality descriptions and are designed to reduce things to a manageable level. As you will see when we examine questionnaires, this usually means reducing personality to about five main aspects, or what are usually called 'dimensions'.

Type theories place people in fixed categories – for example, from time to time we may describe someone as being extroverted. When we do this we put the person into a distinct category, and in this case, can probably describe many different characteristics of extroverted people. It is a common way of describing people, so we all know more or less what we mean. Of course, the problem with doing this is that many people do not conveniently fall into one category or another – some people may be a mixture of both extroversion and introversion.

To help solve this problem, trait theories allow someone to be described by their scores on a number of dimensions, each dimension applying to a different trait. (A 'trait' is just an aspect of someone's personality which, compared to another person, they possess to a greater or lesser extent.) Clearly, this approach allows for all sorts of different combinations of traits and for an individual to be anywhere on a particular dimension. Thus, while extroversion and introversion may be at opposite ends, you can be anywhere on the dimension, including the middle.

In some ways, the distinction between types and traits really doesn't matter in that they are both ways of making sense of personality. However, the trait approach does give more room for manoeuvre and allows us to produce a common set of traits against which we can all be compared. It does more to illustrate the vast range of different personalities and is fairer than simply categorising people. But be warned, traits describe what we are like; they do not explain how we came to be the way we are.

Do you know yourself?

So far, the question has been about the possible origins of personality, but we do have a sense of our own personalities. We can all think of events that have altered out view of the world and have changed the way in which we behave towards other people. As adults, usually, we have also developed ways of coping with our own personality. A good example would be someone who has to talk in public as part of his job, but who is really not a very extroverted person. Inside he may feel uncomfortable about having to do it, but at a practical level he will have developed ways of coping with the experience. So he quells his nerves by preparing what he is going to say with great care, considering carefully the questions people might ask and arriving early to get acquainted with the venue.

Thus, the way in which we cope with our personalities is frequently based on what we know about ourselves. However, most of us do not have a full or clear picture of what we are really like. This may be because we do not know how to describe ourselves, or it may be because we try to ignore what we suspect we might be like. Whatever the reason, it is actually very informative to sit down and describe yourself.

What follows is an exercise that will start you on the process of finding out what you are like and what other people think you are like.

The self-discovery exercise

1. Find a blank piece of paper and write down ten adjectives that you feel describe your personality. Make sure they are about your personality and are not words describing your appearance. Try to complete the exercise in ten minutes. *If you get stuck, there is a list of trait adjectives at the end of this chapter.*

2. Now find someone who knows you well and get them to write down ten words that also describe your personality. *Do not show them your list first.*

3. After about ten minutes, stop your friend or partner and compare the two lists. How have you described yourself? Was it difficult to find ten words? What has your friend written down? Do you agree with each other? What are the differences?

If you have completed the exercise, you will probably find that the way in which you see yourself is not identical to how other people see you. Furthermore, the two people involved knew quite a lot about you! What would an employer do?

It is actually quite difficult to describe yourself accurately. In a similar way you can probably also think of situations where you did something you would not have predicted – ie, you failed to predict your own behaviour. It seems that, as individuals, we all have a sense of *not* being aware of every aspect of our own character. Some aspects actually seem to be hidden away and we are not conscious of them. Likewise, it is difficult to describe other people as we tend to pay far too much attention to personal stereotypes – eg, big men are aggressive. In reality, these stereotypes are examples of our own personal, and frequently inaccurate, personality theories. However, what is more important is that those whose job it is to assess your personality also have their own theories. This is one extremely good reason for having an objective method of measuring personality – the personality questionnaire.

Key points

- Personality is influenced by genetic factors and life experience.
- Personality guides your behaviour in particular directions.
- Personality theories are concerned with predicting your *likely* behaviour.
- Type theories put you in particular personality categories – eg, extroverted or introverted.
- Trait theories place you on a number of personality dimensions – eg, degree of extroversion or introversion.

- We are not conscious of every aspect of our own personalities.
- Most of us are not very skilled at describing our own personalities.

The self-discovery exercise: example trait adjectives

Absent-minded	Charitable	Driven
Abstract	Competitive	Dutiful
Accommodating	Compliant	Efficient
Achieving	Composed	Emotional
Affable	Conceptual	Empathic
Affectionate	Confident	Enterprising
Affiliative	Conscientious	Enthusiastic
Aggravating	Consoling	Expedient
Altruistic	Contesting	Experimenting
Ambitious	Controlled	Explicit
Amicable	Controlling	Expressive
Analytical	Conventional	Extroverted
Animated	Co-operative	Fearful
Antagonistic	Creative	Flexible
Anxious	Critical	Forceful
Apprehensive	Cynical	Formal
Argumentative	Decisive	Forthright
Artistic	Defensive	Genial
Assertive	Deferential	Gentle
Attentive	Democratic	Genuine
Aware	Determined	Gregarious
Benevolent	Diplomatic	Guarded
Blithe	Direct	Hasty
Blunt	Disciplined	Hesitant
Bold	Discreet	Hostile
Calm	Disorganised	Humble
Candid	Distant	Hurried
Capricious	Docile	Hypothetical
Caring	Dominant	Imaginative
Cautious	Domineering	Impetuous
Changeable	Doubting	Impulsive

Incisive	Phlegmatic	Steady
Inconsistent	Planful	Strategic
Independent	Playful	Stressed
Informal	Practical	Striving
Inhibited	Pragmatic	Structured
Innovative	Precise	Stubborn
Inquiring	Predictable	Subjective
Inquisitive	Private	Submissive
Inspired	Proactive	Suspicious
Intense	Prompt	Systematic
Introspective	Pushy	Temperamental
Introverted	Quarrelsome	Tenacious
Intuitive	Radical	Tender
Involved	Rash	Tense
Irrational	Rational	Tidy
Irresponsible	Reactive	Timid
Jolly	Realistic	Tolerant
Lethargic	Rebellious	Tough
Listless	Reflective	Trusting
Literal	Relaxed	Uncompromising
Lively	Reliable	Undisciplined
Loyal	Repressed	Unexacting
Modest	Reserved	Unorthodox
Neat	Restless	Unrestrained
Neurotic	Restrained	Unselfish
Obedient	Retiring	Unsentimental
Optimistic	Rigid	Unworried
Organised	Ruthless	Venturesome
Original	Satisfied	Vigilant
Ostentatious	Selfless	Vital
Outgoing	Sensing	Vulnerable
Outspoken	Sensitive	Warm
Perceptive	Sensuous	Wary
Perfectionist	Shrewd	Wilful
Persuasive	Shy	Willing
Perturbable	Sober	Yielding
Pessimistic	Stable	Zealous

Note: All the adjectives in the above list are used in real personality questionnaires.

2

How is Personality Measured?

The history of personality measurement stretches back thousands of years. In fact, one of the earliest examples is provided by Gideon who saved the people of Israel from the Midianites. His army recruitment officers shortlisted soldiers by the simple device of asking any who were afraid to return home. Those who were left were then asked to drink from a stream. The soldiers who cupped the water in their hands, enabling them to notice an attacking force, were selected for their quality of alertness, unlike those who bent down and drank directly from the stream. Interestingly, this quality of 'awareness' is still important today and is a feature of some psychological testing systems designed for military selection.

Body humours

Another early example of personality classification is provided by Hippocrates who lived around 400BC. He was a Greek thinker who developed a theory of personality based on what were known as body humours. Hippocrates believed that the four humours were body fluids, which were present in different proportions in different people, the balance of one against another determining a particular personality or temperament. The humours were also linked to the four elements – earth, air, fire and water – which were thought to make up the fabric of the universe.

Humour	Element	Temperament	Behaviour
Blood	Air	Sanguine	Hopeful, confident, optimistic
Black bile	Earth	Melancholic	Depressed, dejected, fearful
Yellow bile	Fire	Choleric	Aggressive, energetic, irritable
Phlegm	Water	Phlegmatic	Self-possessed, lazy, apathetic

Looking at this theory today, we can see that it is far too simple to explain all the different personalities that we encounter. Psychologists also know that while there are some aspects of body biochemistry that influence personality, the ones in the above list are not the right ones! For example, extroversion appears to be related to the 'arousability' of the central nervous system; or, to put it another way, extroverts need higher levels of stimulation to activate their brains and so actively seek out other people and potentially exciting situations.

The body humour theory of personality held sway for many centuries. People would occasionally add to it, and at one stage it was also related to physical appearance. Indeed, if you have read the last chapter, this idea should remind you of Sheldon's 'body build' theory. It may also remind you of the ancient art of phrenology, whereby personality is determined by examining the shape and surface of a person's skull – the bumps on the top of the head – and palmistry, whereby a person's character is read by looking at the crease lines on their hands.

These physical characteristic methods are interesting, but unfortunately are not founded on anything that is provable scientifically. However, you should note that there are some aspects of a person that can be determined by examining their physical characteristics. For example, the form and condition of the fingers and finger nails can give clues to particular medical conditions. The other main reason for being aware of the influence of appearance is that it is how we all judge other people. Thus it should be no surprise that physical attractiveness is a crucial factor in all types of interpersonal relationships, including, of course, the interview.

Projective tests

Moving forward to more scientific approaches, the first objective way of testing personality, the ink blot test, will be familiar to many people through films and television. The most famous test of this type was designed by Rorschach, a Swiss psychiatrist, who developed a way of assessing personality by showing people a series of ink blots. The different interpretations people placed on the ink patterns demonstrated their different personality characteristics.

The Rorschach method is an example of the so-called projective technique in that the client 'projects' his thoughts on to a series of ink blots. The blots themselves do not have, in fact, any deliberate structure – ie, they are not designed to look like a horse, a ship, or whatever might be 'seen' in the blot. In this way, they are quite unlike personality questionnaires in which you are asked to respond to usually quite obvious sets of questions.

The way in which ink blot tests are scored is rather obscure and extremely complicated. The following details are noted:

- **Location.** Did you use a bit of the ink blot or the whole thing?
- **Determinants.** How did you respond to form, colour, shading and any apparent 'movement'?

- **Content.** Did you see human figures, parts of the body, animals, inanimate objects or symbols?
- **Frequency.** Did your responses fall into particular categories – eg, animal or human forms?

While this is a popular way of measuring personality in some countries, it is relatively little used in the UK, mainly because the answers require very skilled interpretation. Furthermore, people do not find it an acceptable or realistic way of being assessed. This is an important practical issue as people tend to react against approaches that they cannot understand directly. Whether the test actually works or not then becomes secondary as people begin to believe that it smacks of black magic. This is a pity because tests of this sort can work very well, and the proof is actually whether it really does predict your personality. However, you should still be on your guard because it is quite easy to produce something that appears to work. The sort of personality 'tests' you find in popular magazines fall into this category. As an example, try the following:

The colour test

Your favourite colours reflect your personality. They can also have a very powerful effect on how you feel, your mood and your general well-being. In fact, research has shown that surrounding yourself with the right colours can increase your work rate and make you feel more satisfied and relaxed.

This test requires you to choose the two colours you like the most, and the one colour you like the least, from a list of 12. Each colour represents a different aspect of personality.

It is important that you decide quickly about the colours and do not spend too much time analysing your choice. Don't associate the colours with clothing or house colour schemes or anything of that nature – just decide which you like the most, and which the least.

The colours are as follows:

Black	☐	Pink	☐
Blue	☐	Purple	☐
Brown	☐	Red	☐
Green	☐	Turquoise (Blue/Green)	☐
Grey	☐	White	☐
Orange	☐	Yellow	☐

1. Pick the colour you like the most from the 12 colours. Put a tick in the box.
2. Pick your next favourite colour from the remaining 11 colours. Put a tick in the box.
3. Now pick the colour you like the least from the remaining 10 colours. Put a cross in the box.
4. Look at the end of this chapter for the meanings of your choices.

Note: We can all have what appears to be contradictory personalities – eg, it is possible to be outgoing in some situations and shy in others.

The colour test is based on research into the effects of colours. For instance, it has been discovered that placing violent people in rooms that are painted pink has a calming effect. Manufacturers also use colours when they are packaging their products. Thus you will hardly ever find sweet foods in green packaging, because green is an astringent or 'drying' colour.

However, before we get carried away with colour psychology, it is something of a leap to suggest that asking you about your colour preferences is a realistic way of finding out about your personality. Indeed, the Colour Test is an example of how easy it is to give the illusion that personality is being measured. That is because it confirms the stereotype personalities we have in mind – ie, those who prefer red are fiery, go-getting and confident, whereas 'green' people are quiet and thoughtful. It also ties in conveniently with how we describe our feelings: 'seeing red', 'green with envy', 'the blues', 'in the pink', and 'in a black mood'.

Before we move away from tests of a projective type, it is useful to mention two other related methods. The first is the Sentence Completion test in which people are presented with the first part of a sentence that they are asked to complete every quickly – eg:

'I am ...'   ... happy, strong, worried
'I am afraid of ...' ... other people, falling, spiders
'I want to be ...'   ... successful, rich, alone

Just like the Rorschach method, the idea is that you project your immediate thoughts on to the sentence and so reveal your deep-rooted, or unconscious, self.

The other method is called Objective Personality Testing. In this approach you are presented with simple tasks that you have to complete quickly. The instructions are, deliberately, slightly incomplete. An example is to be presented with many pairs of numbers and letters, some of which are identical, while others have slight differences. The task is to say rapidly which are the same and which are different:

2B34Y   2B43Y
673GH   673GH
DE76B   DE76E

This has more structure than the other techniques, but the fact that personality is being measured is still obscured. In the example given, the test is actually measuring a person's awareness, or how sensitive they are to small differences in the environment around them.

Whether you believe in them or not, all these techniques are either at the fringe of personality assessment or are relatively little used for selection. Thus, while Objective Personality Tests *are* used for assessing job applicants, they are mostly employed in careers guidance. What this means is that it is another technique, the personality questionnaire, which is the most popular method of measuring personality for selection purposes.

The personality questionnaire

Personality questionnaires are termed self-report measures in that you are asked to describe your personality through the medium of a series of questions. The questions ask about various aspects of your personality and, depending on the sort of questionnaire, allow you to answer in a number of different ways. Some examples are given below:

Example 1

I enjoy public speaking. a) True b) False
This allows you to choose between two options.

Example 2

I like everything to be neat and tidy. a) True b) ? c) False
This allows you to choose between two options or to indicate that you are not sure (?).

Example 3

Which is most like you:
a) I enjoy public speaking.
b) I like everything to be neat and tidy.
This forces you to choose between two statements regardless of whether you think either is relevant. Another approach is to give you blocks of four statements (or sometimes just single words) and ask you to say which is most like you and which is least like you:

I am a person who :
Likes to take risks.   ☐
Prefers to work alone.   ☐
Aims for perfection.   ☐
Enjoys meeting new people.   ☐

Example 4

Indicate how much you agree with each statement:

	Strongly disagree				Strongly agree
I am always early for appointments.	1	2	3	4	5
I have two or three really close friends.	1	2	3	4	5
I work best by myself.	1	2	3	4	5

This allows you to be more precise about your level of agreement with each statement. A similar format is when you are given trait words rather than statements:

	Strongly disagree				Strongly agree
Controlling	1	2	3	4	5
Hesitant	1	2	3	4	5
Tense	1	2	3	4	5

If you are asked to complete a personality questionnaire, you will find that the questions or statements are presented in one of the four formats mentioned. You should also be aware that there are three ways of allowing you to record your answers:

1. **Answer sheet.** You read the questions from a booklet and record your answers with a pencil on a separate answer sheet.
2. **Pocket calculator.** You read the questions from a booklet and enter your answers, using the keyboard, on to a specially programmed pocket calculator.
3. **Computer.** You read the questions from a computer screen and enter your answers using the keyboard.

Computer-based testing is becoming more common, so you should not be surprised to be assessed in this way. With the advent of multi-media computer technology, it is also likely that new tests will be able to use video clips and sound. You should be prepared, therefore, for more interactive, 'game'-like tests.

'The Big Five'

Most personality questionnaires are designed to measure the full range of personality. So, for example, the two best-sellers, the Sixteen Personality Factory questionnaire (16PF™) and the Occupational Personality Questionnaire (OPQ®), measure 16 and 32 aspects of personality respectively (see Chapter 7). However, despite the different number of scales in various questionnaires, it is generally agreed that there are five main aspects or dimensions to personality. These are known by psychologists as 'The Big Five'.

The names given to the five dimensions vary, depending on who designed the questionnaire. Broadly, they can be described as follows:

Extroverted ⇔ Introverted

Extroverts are outgoing, talkative and lively individuals. They tend to be comfortable with strangers and search out company. Introverts are introspective and reserved, and prefer their own company. They prefer to get on with things quietly by themselves.

Tough minded ⇔ Tender minded

Tough-minded people are assertive, energetic and can sometimes appears to be rather insensitive. Tender-minded people are caring and supportive, and put great value on warm and trusting relationships.

Conforming ⇔ Creative

Those who are conforming are down-to-earth and moderate.

They tend to apply common sense to whatever they do. The creative person is more interested in having ideas, practical or not, and may fight against rules and regulations.

High structure ⇔ **Low structure**

Highly structured individuals are precise, formal and methodical. They believe that there is a place for everything and are detail conscious and tidy. Low-structured individuals are casual and spontaneous. They dislike routine and can be disorganised.

Confident ⇔ **Emotional**

Confident people are relaxed and unruffled. They tend to be easy going and can take things in their stride. Emotional people are prone to anxiety and bottle-up their tensions.

In reality, people may be at the extremes of these dimensions or somewhere in between. Fortunately, questionnaires designers are conscious of this, so there are usually scales that run between the 'poles'. For example, it is possible to be a relatively tough-minded person *and* to be caring and empathic when necessary.

Emotional intelligence

An idea that takes the Big Five one step further is the latest thing in personality psychology: emotional intelligence. This can be defined as 'the capacity for recognising our own feelings and those of others, for motivating ourselves, and for managing emotions well, in ourselves and in our relationships'. It is really to do with the notion that intelligence always needs to be accompanied by emotional competence if we are to be truly effective. Indeed, many claim that emotional intelligence is twice as important as IQ or technical expertise; and large companies are getting so excited by the idea that questionnaires that measure emotional intelligence are now routinely being used to identify and develop leaders and to create better teams.

Emotional intelligence questionnaires typically measure:

- *Self-awareness* – how you experience your feelings and your ability to control them.
- *Resilience* – how you perform under pressure and your ability to change your behaviour.
- *Drive* – the amount of energy you have to achieve your goals.
- *Sensitivity* – how aware you are of other people's needs and the degree to which you take such needs into account.
- *Influence* – your ability to bring other people around to your point of view.
- *Decisiveness* – your ability to make clear and unambiguous decisions, even when you may not have all the information you would like.
- *Integrity* – your ability to stick to a course of action and to do what is right.

As you can see these are all factors, or strictly speaking bundles of factors, that are important in any sort of managerial job; and they have been shown to actually predict performance! Indeed, one of the largest consultancy firms has estimated that businesses that commit to the emotional intelligence idea receive an average return on their investment of 1000 per cent – an incredible and probably over-inflated figure, though the emotional intelligence movement is certainly making a splash. Perhaps the best news is that the skills that underpin the concept can be learnt. This is where things differ substantially from plain old intelligence, which changes little after our teenage years, because our emotional competence can change and grow. As Daniel Goleman, the world expert in this area, puts it: there is an old-fashioned word for this sort of growth, maturity.

Another new twist on personality concerns the way we react

when we get 'ragged at the edges', or if you like, what happens when our masks slip. Questionnaires that measure this 'dark side' of a person's personality look at the attributes that tend to undermine trust and loyalty and to get in the way of achieving career goals.

To take an example, a questionnaire called the Hogan Development Survey (HDS), has 11 dark-side scales. It includes a scale 'Charming-Manipulative', which is concerned with the tendency to appear charming, friendly and fun-loving but also impulsive and manipulative. People who get high scores on this scale make a good first impression, but others find them hard to work with because they tend to push things too far, ignore their mistakes and take risks. This sort of behaviour becomes magnified when the 'charmer' is under pressure.

Interestingly work with the HDS has shown that when we are stressed we tend to revert to one of three distinct ways of responding:

- *Moving away from others* – becoming more volatile, mistrustful, careful, detached or (passively) aggressive.
- *Moving against others* – by being more confident or arrogant, manipulative, dramatic and eccentric.
- *Moving towards others* – by becoming more diligent or perfectionist, dutiful and dependent.

This might appear to concentrate on the negative but it is important to realise that not all behaviour is constructive, and that whether or not these sorts of characteristics get in the way of what we want to do depends on our other strengths and competencies.

Psychologists are starting to look at something called 'attributional' style. This concerns the ways in which we attribute causes to the events that happen to us. When styles are examined it seems that there are two main types of people: optimists and pessimists.

Optimists see problems as challenges and opportunities, whereas pessimists anticipate problems and expect the worst. However, the most important distinction between the two is that optimists do not blame themselves, and when something happens they are more likely to attribute it to an external cause and to consider it to be a temporary setback. Likewise, when everything is going well they feel that success is due to their actions, and believe the outcome to be lasting. The situation with pessimists is the complete opposite; they feel that they are victims of circumstance, blame themselves when things go wrong – and unlike optimists – do not take the credit for their successes. As with other aspects of personality, the two types are not in themselves necessarily 'good' or 'bad' – it depends entirely on what a person is trying to do. What do you think the best style for a sales person would be?

Impression management

It may have occurred to you as you have been reading about self-report questionnaires that there is nothing to stop you putting down the answers that you think will do the most good. So if you were applying for a job that required extroverted people, it is unlikely that you would respond positively to all the questions concerning introversion. We all have a natural tendency to present ourselves in the best possible light. This is a big problem in test design and is known variously as 'motivational distortion', 'social desirability, 'impression management' or 'impression control'.

The designers of questionnaires know that we all want to produce a good 'test' performance, and that some of us also answer questions in the way in which we think the psychologist or employer *wants* us to answer. The latter fact is the 'social desirability' aspect of our behaviour.

Practically, there are three solutions to this question. One answer is to use projective tests because we do not know what is expected of us anyway. Another answer is to have special questions that pick up anyone who is attempting to be too good to be true. These are usually a series of questions that have 'right' or 'wrong' answers – eg:

Have you ever told a lie?	a) Yes	b) No
Have you ever done anything risky?	a) Yes	b) No
Have you ever lost your temper?	a) Yes	b) No

Only a saint could answer 'No' to all of these. However, the most effective method is to produce tests in which you have to be consistent, which are also *empirically* based. The consistency comes from having many questions that are concerned with the same dimension. This makes it difficult to distort the results as you have to remember your answers to all the other questions. The empirical aspect is based on statistics. What this means is that you can produce a series of questions, which in themselves do not have to look as if they have anything to do with the aspect of personality being measured, as long as they discriminate statistically between different personalities. For example:

Do you prefer showers to baths?	a) Yes	b) No

In this case the question, along with a number of others, is used in a real personality questionnaire to explore male and female characteristics. What do you think the average male is likely to answer?

In practical terms, you should be conscious that questionnaires contain items that are designed to pick out unusual performances and that it is 'dangerous' to contradict yourself. Also, you should bear in mind that you don't know precisely what the psychologist or employer is looking for in terms of personality. You might distort your results in the wrong direction. For more advice on completing personality questionnaires, see Chapter 4.

Key points

- There are a number of ways of measuring personality, including projective tests, sentence completion tests and objective personality tests.

- The most popular method of measuring personality for job selection purposes is the personality questionnaire.
- Personality questionnaire questions can come in a number of different forms. Some force you to make choices, others allow you to indicate how much you agree with a particular statement.
- You record your answers on paper, pocket calculator or computer – ie, not all questionnaires are 'paper and pencil'.
- There are five main aspects of personality. These are concerned with extroversion vs. introversion; tough-mindedness vs. tender-mindedness; conformity vs. creativity; high structure vs. low structure; and confidence vs. emotionality (see pages 22–23).
- Many personality questionnaires are designed to detect whether you are presenting yourself in an overly positive or 'socially desirable' way.

Interpreting the colour test

Important: this 'test' is for entertainment purposes only.

The following descriptions give the personality characteristics that go with the 12 colours. Look for your two *most preferred* colours and read the descriptions.

When you look for your *least preferred* colour, bear in mind that the description indicates what you are least likely to be like. However, it does not mean that you have none of the characteristics mentioned, just that you are more likely to behave in the way suggested by your most preferred colours.

1. Black
This colour is chosen by people who are confident in themselves. It is a sign of those who strive for success and in many ways is *the* achievement colour. However, it is also a sign of the rejection of authority, and sometimes of a willingness to act without necessarily thinking through all the consequences.

2. Blue
This colour appeals to 'down-to-earth', conventional sorts of people. It is the colour of calmness and is chosen by those looking for peace and tranquillity. 'Blue' people are trustworthy and want organised and orderly environments. Sometimes it is a sign of anxiety.

3. Brown
Like black, this is the colour of achievement. It is also a sign of security and a desire to have 'roots'. 'Brown' people are at ease with themselves and concerned with home comforts. Sometimes indicates a need for fulfilment and a search for contentment.

4. Green
This can be a sign of introversion, but paradoxically, it also indicates a person with a need to impress others. 'Green' people like to be recognised and accepted as having useful contributions to make. They can sometimes be seen as over-bearing or appear to tell other people how to run their lives.

5. Grey
Grey is a safe and neutral colour. It is chosen by people who prefer to keep themselves to themselves. However, sometimes it indicates a deep-rooted desire to impress and to make a mark. Thus 'grey' people frequently compensate by vigorously throwing themselves into social activities.

6. Orange
Orange is a sign of an impulsive and friendly person. It is often selected by those who take life as it comes. The 'orange' person does not worry over little things and may even have a 'fatalist' attitude. It is a vibrant colour and is indicative of a sociable character.

7. Pink
Pink is chosen by those who are caring and passionate. It has obvious romantic overtones, but indicates a somewhat overpowering temperament. The 'pink' person can sometimes crave attention a little too much and tend to swamp other people.

There may also be a tendency to appear to know what is best for others.

8. Purple

Purple is a very powerful colour and indicates a spiritual, yet frequently restless character. It is chosen by those who are searching for meaning or who have an intellectual curiosity for the human condition. It is no accident that purple is often used as the colour for the robes of religious leaders.

9. Red

Red is power. It is the colour of the supremely confident and of those who experience life intensively. 'Red' people are out to win and enjoy competition. It can also indicate a flashy and sometimes insecure character. However, it does have impact, and, stereotypically, is associated with desire and sexual energy.

10. Turquoise

This is an enigmatic colour which represents spiritual energy and renewal. It is a sign of a well-balanced individual who has a sense of his own worth and a feeling for his place in the world. It is an individual choice and sometimes 'turquoise' people can appear a little too relaxed.

11. White

White is chosen by those with a need to express themselves. It is characteristic of people who need to have space to think or experiment. 'White' people can be good at coming up with ideas, but may also be lacking in practicality. White is often associated with purity, but in this sense it is more likely to indicate a lack of wordliness than anything else.

12. Yellow

This colour is chosen by the optimist. It can also be a sign of escape or indicate someone who feels that he has little control over the world around him. 'Yellow' people can be very energetic, but it tends to come in the form of short, sharp bursts of activity. 'Yellow' people are restless for change and can sometimes be accused of changing things for the sake of it.

3

Job Profiles and Personality Reports

When you complete a personality questionnaire, your results are compared with a large group of other people who have completed the same questionnaire under the same conditions. This is because the scores on a personality questionnaire are only meaningful for selection purposes when you compare them with the scores of other people. The results in themselves have no pre-determined significance and must be evaluated against this normative group. The comparison allows the psychologist or employer to see precisely how your performance compares on all the scales or dimensions used in the questionnaire. Once all the results are standardised in this way, a further comparison can be made with the people who completed the questionnaire in the same session as yourself – ie, the other applicants for the job.

Another reason for these comparisons is that your personality results are compared with the ideal profile for the job or position in question. The ideal profile is drawn up by a personnel specialist and is based on the following sorts of information:

- An analysis of what the current occupant(s) of the job actually does. This is usually in terms of the specialist knowledge required to do the job, any skills or abilities that are needed, and the ideal personality. It sometimes involves watching people actually performing their jobs.
- An examination of the existing job description. Which factors were identified as important the last time that the job was analysed? Naturally, while this can provide some useful background information, most job descriptions are woefully out of date.
- A prediction of the future demands of the job. This is the trickiest part of the analysis and depends on deciding whether new skills will be needed or whether people with different sorts of personality will be required.

All of this information is put together to produce a picture of the best person for the job. However, in many cases the perfect person does not exist. So the profile also has to indicate which features are more important than others, and the range of characteristics that are allowable. The latter is a crucial point and usually means that more than one personality is going to be suitable for any given job. This is good news for the job hunter.

To give an idea of the sorts of profiles that are used, four typical examples follow. These pick out aspects of the main personality dimensions that have been identified as being particularly important.

Managerial profile

Psychologists have expended a great deal of energy on identifying a 'good' managerial profile. It seems that, in personality terms, your managerial or supervisory potential is enhanced if you are:

Willing to assume responsibility

Effective managers like assuming responsibility, and get satisfaction from organising and motivating staff. They see business performance as being a group effort, but can also use a forceful and direct approach when appropriate. In many cases, what this amounts to is leadership style, because leaders are concerned with achieving results through other people. However, there are at least five ways, or different patterns of behaviour, by which a leader can achieve results. These are:

1. **Direction.** This is where a leader makes all the rules and takes responsibility for all the decision making. This is also known as the 'autocratic' style.
2. **Delegation.** In this case the decision making is made by other people and the responsibility is shared. The leader takes a 'back-seat' role and delegates control.
3. **Participation.** A participative leader seeks out the opinions of other people and actively tries to involve everyone in decision making.
4. **Consultation.** This approach involves paying close attention to the thoughts and feelings of other people, but the leader still makes the final decisions.
5. **Negotiation.** This is about making deals with other people. It is an 'I'll scratch your back, if you'll scratch my back' approach.

These are all reasonable ways of getting people to do things, but some will be better than others, depending on the circumstances. In particular, the most effective style will be influenced by the size of the organisation. For example, it is not easy to make *all* the decisions in a large company. Also, the personalities of a leader's subordinates need to be taken into account; a truly delegative style, for instance, would not be appropriate if others are unhappy to make their own decisions.

People orientated and confident

This shows itself in an ability to deal with people at all levels. It is also related to negotiation skills and persuasiveness. These are important for areas such as sales and any situation that requires one person to influence another actively. As with leadership style, this really centres on working with and through other people. People orientation is all about having an active interest in what makes people 'tick', and being able to gain their respect and confidence. This relies on the ability to 'read' other people's behaviour, to understand what concerns and motivates them, and then to respond in the most appropriate way. The really skilled manager will be able to do this *despite* his natural leadership style.

Flexible and able to respond

These factors suggest that good managers are able to cope with change and to react quickly to new business opportunities. The ability to respond to change is especially important as the pace of business life quickens. However, that is not to say that high levels of flexibility are necessarily a good thing. Thus, while most situations demand a degree of flexibility, if you are flexible about everything, little will get done. Some psychologists call the latter the 'butterfly syndrome' because it neatly describes the way in which some people flit from one thing to another, never settling on anything. Very high levels of flexibility also tend to be associated with those who get bored easily, and dislike routine and repetitive tasks.

Decisive and results-driven

This is all about getting the job done. In business, it is extremely important to make the right decisions at the right time and to have an eye on the end product. Producing the goods or service on time also requires the ability to plan ahead.

Planning itself can be looked at in a number of different ways. Technically, it is possible to draw a distinction between tactical planning, which is the day-to-day process of achieving set goals, and strategic planning, which is the long-term process of deciding where an organisation is going and of visualising how it is going to get there. Indeed, in American management parlance, strategic planning is sometimes known as 'visioning'. However, whatever you want to call it, the ideal manager has the ability to perform both sorts of planning.

Self-promoting

Successful managers promote themselves. This is a question of being relatively tough minded and not too modest. It is a matter of 'blowing your own trumpet' and making sure that people recognise the value of your contribution to an organisation. Unfortunately, many people feel uncomfortable about presenting themselves in this way and tend to get overlooked. Yet to get promoted you do need to market yourself. It is also an uncomfortable fact that those who are made redundant from jobs tend to lack the ability to sell themselves while they are in the job.

Sales profile

If any job is reliant on personality it is sales. This is the activity *par excellence* that depends on interpersonal skills and a 'winning' personality. Sales performance is influenced by your ability to:

Respond in a warm and open manner

This is a question of reacting appropriately and appearing to be genuine (not oozing insincerity). You can teach people to appear warm and genuine, but natural sales people seem to have these features in-built. To state the obvious, you also have to be interested in people and human behaviour.

If you have ever experienced an expert sales presentation, you may remember how painless it seemed. However, you probably don't recall much of the detail, apart from the fact that the conversation was perfectly plausible. This is because your behaviour was being assessed and your 'objections' were dealt with almost before you had time to articulate them. Indeed, what was happening is that the sales pitch was designed to synchronise with your unspoken questions – eg:

Why should I listen?	*Sales pitch: Description of the benefit of the product.*
What is the product?	*Sales pitch: A fuller description of the product.*
What do I get out of it?	*Sales pitch: The direct benefit to you.*
Can this be true?	*Sales pitch: The evidence and reasons for the benefits.*
Ah, but ...	*Sales pitch: Your objections preempted and dealt with.*
Can I check the facts?	*Sales pitch? Summary of the product and benefits again.*

In the hands of a skilled operator who is genuinely sensitive to your reactions, this sequence can prove highly effective.

Appear confident

This is similar to the confidence required to be a good manager, but is reinforced by the need to be resilient to customers. For example, you need to be able to cope with knock-backs, criticism and outright rudeness. It is a fact that you are not going to sell much if you don't bounce back quickly. To be precise, the sort of confidence that is required is 'public' confidence. This is really an aspect of extroversion in that it involves being able to approach people easily and to be at ease with them, regardless of what happens. Interestingly, this contrasts with the sort of confidence that makes you think you are right, or what is termed self-assuredness. This is a quiet and non-demonstrative confidence, which is useful for getting a job done, but is not what is needed to get your foot in the door in the first place.

Be sensitive

If it is a question of selling somebody something, you must be aware of what is going on. This means picking up whether the customer is actually interested in what you are saying and of being sensitive to the general atmosphere. We have already looked a this in terms of responding to other people. However, you should realise that, used in this way, 'sensitive' does not mean being concerned for other people's feelings; rather, it implies that you are able to detect what somebody is thinking and to act on what you find.

Think quickly

This is all about 'thinking on your feet'. You must be able to cope with rapidly changing situations and, for example, to be able to calculate improved offers 'off the cuff'. This requires the co-operation of the mouth and the brain! It is also a skill that comes through practice. If you think back to our expert sales pitch, the reason that it works is that it is well-practised. No doubt it also involves a great deal of natural talent as well. Yet the point is that the acquisition of any skill, including presentational skills such as selling, generally requires a good deal of hard work. Indeed, if you have had experience in this area, you will recognise that the process of perfecting a skill can be broken down into a number of stages:

1. **Ignorance.** This is when you think that something looks easy and you don't realise how much work is involved – the 'there's nothing to it' stage.
2. **Realisation.** This is sometimes called 'conscious incompetence' and is when you realise how hard it really is – eg, you try to copy someone and you cannot.
3. **Competence.** This involves a great deal of effort because now you realise that you have to concentrate on many things at the same time – eg, with sales presentations, on listening, eye contact, body posture, reacting to customer cues, putting your case, countering arguments, etc.
4. **Expertise.** At this stage the technique comes naturally and without effort. In time, however, the expert can become careless and complacent (and start to sound insincere). He should return to the 'competence' stage and retrain!

All of the above points, including the process of acquiring presentation skills, are components of being 'persuasive'. This is perhaps the one word that sums up the effective sales person. On the other hand, the problem with the sales profile is that most salespeople tend to show low conformity and low structure. This means that they don't like rules and regulations, and can be somewhat disorganised.

Entrepreneurial profile

Given the increasing number of people who start their own businesses, another profile that has received considerable attention is that of the entrepreneur. This is not only of interest to those thinking of starting their own ventures, but to banks and venture capitalists as well – after all, they lend the money. The classic entrepreneurial profile includes:

Perseverance

This is one of the most important factors, as running a business is frequently an exercise in unrelenting persistence. If you examine how famous entrepreneurs started, you find that most have 'failed' many times before they hit on a successful formula. It is a question of trying until the formula emerges.

Perseverance is closely linked to the source of entrepreneurs' inspiration – ie, where they find their business ideas and how they develop them. Research has shown that successful entrepreneurs use many different sources of information and work hard to test their ideas. It also seems that the most innovative entrepreneurs tend to assess information by looking for what makes one thing different from another. This is in contrast to the behaviour of most people, who tend naturally to fit new ideas into existing categories or to pigeonhole information.

Moderate risk-taking

Contrary to popular opinion, most entrepreneurs are not wild risk-takers. There is, of course, an element of risk in setting up a business, but that risk has been calculated very carefully. In this respect entrepreneurs are not gamblers, but neither do they shy away from risking their livelihoods for the sake of a good idea.

Entrepreneurs rarely make a mistake in their risk-taking based on the law of probability. The classic example of this sort of mistake is the 'gambler's fallacy', whereby the chances of something happening in the future is confused with what has happened in the past. For example, you put your money on five horse races and lose each time, but you believe that if you can only keep going your luck will be bound to change because you are *due* a win. Unfortunately, this is complete nonsense because past events, in this sense, do not influence future events (bookmakers and casino owners will never tell you this). Entrepreneurs, it seems, can weigh up risks without falling into such a trap.

A need to achieve

Most people want to achieve something and to be successful, but entrepreneurs are *driven* by the need to create a successful business. This is really an extreme form of competition and is similar, for example, to the desire a sales person might have to be the top performer in an organisation. Thus, entrepreneurs are definitely out to win. There may also be an element of showing other people what they can do. Despite this, it is essentially a personal behaviour pattern, because the highest standards to live up to are often your own. The reason behind this is that once you have reached your goal, you move the goalposts forward. It is similar to climbing to the top of a mountain only to discover that it is one peak among many higher peaks.

Self-control

In the entrepreneurial sense, this is what psychologists call an 'internal locus of control' meaning that you believe that you control events and are responsible for your own destiny rather than events being imposed on you by other people and society at large. This confirms the fact that entrepreneurs are not fatalists. They believe that they are in control and, moreover, that they can influence other people. The control factor is interesting and is reflected in the way in which entrepreneurs tend to manage businesses as they get larger. Most entrepreneurs are happy to run a small business because they can control every aspect of it, but they are less successful with a larger operation because some aspects of control have to be relinquished. This can be difficult for the entrepreneur who usually identifies very closely with his business. So when the centre of power starts to shift away from him, the entrepreneur frequently moves on to a new business idea.

Independence

Entrepreneurs have a strong desire to be independent. Some-times this can make them appear to be egocentric and selfish. In a similar way to the managerial profile, the entrepreneur needs to be single-minded and less modest than most people, but running a successful business depends on self-promotion.

Independence, or the wish to be your own boss, is generally the prime reason for starting any sort of business. Psychologically, it is the most strongly held value and is often accompanied by the need for recognition. Other reasons for wanting to be independent are the ability to use your imagina-tion (to be creative); to be responsible for your own life; and last, but not least, to make money for yourself rather than someone else.

Other factors also make the entrepreneur successful in busi-ness, including the ability to cope with change and uncertainty. However, the entrepreneurial profile is not completely unique. The same sort of characteristics are seen in successful sportsmen and women, mountain climbers, and many others.

Technical profile

This final profile concerns those who are involved in technical, scientific or very detailed activities. This could also be described as the 'researcher' profile. It includes a requirement to be:

Personally confident

Technical jobs require a good measure of personal confidence or a belief that you are right. This is important from the point of view of getting the job done and of being sufficiently moti-vated to do it in the first place. This sort of confidence contrasts with the public confidence ('chutzpah') required for sales activities. Personal confidence is also linked to aspects of introversion – in particular, the ability to complete tasks quietly without antagonising others. This is frequently coupled with a good sense of timing and a certain shrewdness in presenting ideas to other people.

Highly structured

This means being very organised and detail conscious. Technical jobs often involve keeping meticulous and detailed records, thus requiring an appropriate sort of mentality. Someone who has a short attention span and who loses interest quickly is unlikely to make a good technician or scientist.

The systematic and orderly way in which technical people go about their jobs is often mirrored in the manner in which they manage their personal lives. Thus, relationships may be dealt with in the same predetermined way and with great attention to detail.

Persistent

Similar to the entrepreneurial profile, any technical activity requires persistence, and a calm and persevering approach. This is related to personal confidence because a dogged determination is required. However, the difficulty with being a highly persistent person is that it is sometimes difficult to know when to stop. This is because it is possible to get so entrenched with the detail that the ultimate objective moves out of sight. In extreme cases, people can be so tenacious that they actively fight against a change of course.

Conforming

Technical activities are not concerned with going off at a tangent (unlike, maybe, invention). Rather they are concerned with taking a logical, analytical and 'conservative' approach to problems. This implies a thoroughness and an ability to follow a problem through right to the end. Conformance also suggests the desire to keep to a given set of rules and regulations, and the wish to work in an environment in which there are no sudden changes. These factors make the technical person quite unlike the sales or entrepreneurial types described earlier, as both of these can cope with measures of ambiguity and uncertainty. Interestingly, the technical profile does not include any straight interpersonal factors. Although they are important – it is vital, of course, for information to be communicated to other people – technical activities tend to be solitary. In this way they require people who are not always actively looking for someone to talk to or for a group of people with which to socialise.

Personality reports

The end product of a personality assessment is a report. For most purposes one will be prepared for each person who completed the questionnaire, and will be used as the basis for comparison with the 'ideal' profile. Reports come in various lengths and obviously differ in the amount of information they contain. For example, a report for a 'Big Five' questionnaire will run to about four sides of A4 paper, whereas a full-length questionnaire might be two or three times as long. The report that follows is an example of a short summary of a person's personality characteristics; the OPQ32® report provided at the end of the book is a good illustration of a full-length 'manager's' report. The latter is worth reading carefully, as it will give you an idea of the sort of detail that is available to employers or those using questionnaires for development purposes.

Example personality report

Mind Style Questionnaire Report

Version 1.2
Candidate X

Introduction

This report provides an analysis of the Mind Style Questionnaire (MSQ) you completed on [date]. The MSQ is used to provide information on your personality that is useful in the selection process. Practically it is used with your application form or curriculum vitae (CV), and any other relevant information, to compare you objectively with the appropriate employment profile.

The MSQ is a self-report questionnaire, which assesses five main aspects, or dimensions, of personality. It gives you the opportunity to describe how you see your own work related behaviour. It is important to realise that it is not a test of intelligence or ability; rather it allows predictions to be made about how you might react under particular circumstances.

To give as full a picture as possible of your personality, your results have been compared with a representative sample of people who have completed the questionnaire in the past. This is called the normative group. In your case, the norm group used is a general sample of the UK working population.

The contents of this report should provide an accurate assessment of your personality for about 18 months, depending on how your working career develops and on your personal circumstances. However, you should realise that no assessment is infallible and that the accuracy of the results depends on the openness of the person completing the questionnaire. Also, as with any psychometric measure, the results should always be used in conjunction with other reliable and valid sources of information.

Your questionnaire results

← − scores	6	5	4	3	2	1	0	1	2	3	4	5	6	+ scores →
Extroverted											■			Introverted
Tough minded										■				Tender minded
Conforming											■			Creative
High structure		■												Low structure
Confident								■						Emotional
Impression control								■						

Interpersonal approach

Extroverted – introverted. Your results suggest that you can be quite a cautious and retiring person. You can be rather analytic when dealing with other people and are more comfortable when you know them well. You probably prefer to work quietly by yourself in a calm atmosphere, rather than work in a busy, noisy environment under a great deal of time pressure.

You can be particularly single-minded and are happy organising your own work. You are also the sort of person who likes to work out for yourself what needs to be done, rather than continually ask other people. In a group situation, you are likely to be viewed as a source of well-thought-out arguments, but are unlikely to want to lead the discussion or to confront other people. You probably won't voice your opinion on a matter unless you have considered things very carefully beforehand.

Tough minded – tender minded. You are the sort of person who likes to achieve things by agreement. You tend to put other people first and to be seen as a warm and caring person. While you may recognise that you are not a particularly outgoing person, people tend to seek you out to talk through their problems and they value your judgement. You are seen as a good listener who is concerned for others.

On occasions, you take a back seat role rather too readily and let other people sway arguments, even though you may know better. This means that you probably work best in a relatively non-competitive workplace rather than in an organisation which is very 'political'.

Work style

Conforming – creative. You tend to like working in places where there is plenty of variety. You like inventing new ways of doing things and of being able to use new ideas. However, you still recognise the value of tried and tested methods, as you use these in conjunction with less conventional methods. If you are forced to do things in a particular way, you sometimes feel a little restricted and stifled.

High structure – Low structure. You are a very organised and detail-conscious person. You tend to approach tasks only after you have thought through what you should do and have prioritised the main parts. However, sometimes the standards you set for yourself, and other people, are too exacting. On occasions, people probably describe you as a perfectionist.

Your organisational skills mean that you fulfil tasks as promised and are recognised as being efficient and accurate. You like your office or working space to be neat, tidy and uncluttered. If you are required to work with disorganised people, it can make you feel tense.

Emotional control

Confident – Emotional. Most of the time you feel reasonably confident and certain of yourself. However, there are times, especially when you are faced with completely new situations, when you feel that your abilities may not be up to the job. Unlike some people, you are unlikely to ride over your problems and you may worry about them.

You are happiest when you have clear-cut goals and are working within a clearly defined organisational structure. Paradoxically, this allows you to be experimental and to try new ideas without feeling stressed. On the other hand, when you have to perform in ambiguous situations you feel uneasy. In such circumstances you are unlikely to take risks and will avoid experiences that you know will make you feel pressured.

Impression control

The MSQ contains a number of questions that identify the extent to which you have intended to present yourself in an overly favourable light. This is a perfectly normal reaction to a personality questionnaire as we all want to do our best. However, sometimes what you do can inflate the results and make them more extreme than they really are.

In your case, the responses indicate that you have answered the questions in a realistic manner and have not felt under pressure to present yourself in a socially desirable way.

The reports produced as part of an employment selection exercise are usually generated by computer. Once your answers have been inputted, the report can be ready and printed in a matter of minutes. Obviously, this is a very quick and economical way for an employer to have personality information ready before an interview. However, it is an unfortunate fact that such computer systems are sometimes in the hands of the unskilled. Furthermore, many people tend to believe, in an unquestioning way, computer-generated reports. This is perhaps not surprising as such reports usually have a very technical and scientific look. Sometimes the most gullible people are those who should know best – personnel managers.

Rogue reports

An illustration of the power of computer-generated reports is an exercise conducted by the author at *the* major yearly personnel services exhibition in the UK. As part of the exhibition it was decided to set up a computer system that 'read' a person's personality from his business card. This was by way of a gimmick as it is obviously not possible to determine a person's personality from information on a card.

To use the system, a client placed his cards in a machine that looked vaguely like a prop from *The Man from UNCLE* and, a few seconds later, accompanied by some whirring noises and a screen full of information on radioactivity levels, pH, salinity, torsional stiffness and aura segmentation, a report came out of a printer. In fact, exactly the same report came out regardless of the input. When the personnel and training managers who had inserted their cards were asked if they thought the report was accurate, a rather worrying number said that they felt it was. Indeed, of the 189 people 'tested', about 40 per cent believed that the results were an accurate reflection of their personality. This was in spite of the fact that the report was concocted in such a way that it contained some bizarre statements so that people would *not* take it seriously. Naturally, everyone who took part had the deception explained to them. However, the results can only be described as unsettling.

The redeeming part to this story is that if you are subject to a computer-based assessment run by a major employer, then you are probably reasonably safe. The chances are that your profile will be interpreted by a properly trained person because virtually all the publishers of personality questionnaires, including those which are presented on computer, require users to be trained to the standards laid down by the British Psychological

Society. In addition, many also demand attendance on their own specialist courses. But be warned, as a potential job candidate, there are systems on the market that do not work and that are in the hands of the untrained.

The business card report:

BUSINESS CARD DISCRIMINATION SYSTEM
Mercantile Report Pro-5

Name: **Organisation:**

Argot interpretation	= 0.3'	**Synthetic**
Icon size	= 0.046	**Maximum 0.07**
Semantic standard	= 2	**Dictionary normal**
Line difference	= 0.23	**Range: 0.15**
Element skew	= 4	**No elements distorted**
Size ratio	= 7	**Asymmetric**

Profile parameters:
Level:

The Barnum score has a 0.05 tolerance. The overall level is 70 per cent, indicating average to high intelligence (UK general), with high verbal (V3) and social skills (Et).

Scale summaries

Social interaction. In general, you are an outgoing individual with well-developed social skills and able to communicate with people at all levels. However, there is a situational component, and sometimes you may feel less confident internally than you appear to be outwardly. Such ergic tension may make you more forthright, more reserved than normal, or both. When you are in an interpersonal guest role, there is a strong indication that you prefer to drink white wine rather than red or rosé.

Thinking style. You can be an imaginative and conceptual thinker. There is a high level of latent ability, but it is probable that you have not yet put it to full use. In development terms, there is a great deal of potential that may well be manifest in terms of managerial progression (promotion), or at a more entrepreneurial level. Your bit capacity appears to be normal, although on occasions you may forget where you have put your car keys.

Stability. You are a stable individual with no major aberrant indicators. There may be occasions when you feel pressured and frustrated, but these can be mediated by your well-developed coping mechanisms. There is no indication of major defence blocks. Now may be a good time for you to take a holiday in Monaco or Andorra.

Work approach. You are a highly motivated individual who has the ability to work well in most situations. However, projects need to engage your interest and there are occasions when you would like to have more variety in your day-to-day work. In general, you are a strong-minded character who likes plenty to do, but occasionally you bite off more than you can chew. You should consult others and give yourself time to digest new ideas.

Type:
Beta. Typical beta types are psychologists, personnel managers, training managers and human resource specialists. Other related: business (non-quantitative), the media, health and the musical world (especially lute players).

Char. Ambitious, outgoing (EPI emulation +), socially skilled, achievement orientated (n.Ach +), internal locus of control (Rotter +), resilient, low ego drift.

Card. The wood pulp, which constitutes 83.5 per cent of this card, came from a 20m high Silva Spruce that grew 36km to the northwest of Oslo.

Important: This report is intended for entertainment purposes only.

Acknowledgement: The business card report was first published in *The Psychologist*, The Bulletin of the British Psychological Society, Volume 6, August 1993.

If you have read the report, no doubt you have drawn your own conclusions. However, we are all sometimes blinded by science, and, after all, personnel managers are only human.

Key points

- Your personality questionnaire results are standardised by comparing them to a representative group of people who have completed the same questionnaire in the past.
- Personnel managers and psychologists analyse jobs to draw up the ideal personality profile for a particular position.
- Different jobs have different 'ideal' profiles. This means that whatever your personal personality profile, it might well fit a number of jobs.
- Questionnaire results are often used to generate assessment reports. Many reports comment on 'The Big Five' personality dimensions (see Chapter 2).
- Computer-generated reports can be misinterpreted; sometimes even professionals are blinded by science.

4

Preparing for Personality Questionnaires

If you apply for a job and are accepted for an interview as a result of what you say in your curriculum vitae (CV) or on your application form, the next stage is typically a psychological assessment. In most cases, this will entail a number of ability tests and a personality questionnaire.

Most employers use two or three distinct sorts of timed ability tests. The first is usually a test of verbal ability and is designed to find out how well you understand the meanings of different words, or whether you can solve logic problems by analysing short passages of information. The second will be a test of numerical ability, which explores your arithmetic skills, or your capabilities with regard to mathematical problems based on tables or charts of information. Finally, but not always, you will be asked to complete a test of perceptual ability. This presents problems in the form of symbols or diagrams and you have to work out the relationships between them.

Clearly, verbal and numerical tests are used to assess your level of literacy and numeracy, both abilities being seen as the key to the effective performance of most sorts of jobs. The perceptual test, which is used less frequently, is valuable for assessing 'non-verbal' reasoning. This is an important factor in problem solving based on direct observation – eg, the practical aspects of science and engineering.

The ability testing part of an assessment can take between one and two hours. The next step is the personality questionnaire. The first thing to realise about this part of the process is that personality questionnaires are untimed. This means that the test administrator is not going to put you under time pressure or use a stopwatch to start and stop you. However, while the questionnaire may be untimed, the administrator will know roughly how long people take. For example, most short questionnaires take about 10 minutes to complete, whereas longer versions can take between 30 and 45 minutes.

Completing a personality questionnaire

Most questionnaires are administered in a standard way to a group of applicants. This means that you will find yourself in a large room seated in rows with possibly up to 30 or 40 other people. The following is a typical sequence of events:

- A trained test administrator will introduce you to the questionnaire. Remember that as this may be after a number of ability tests, you may be a little tired. Make sure that you listen to the instructions.
- The administrator will explain the reasons for the test session, if this has not already been done. The introduction will then include an instruction not to talk while you are completing the test, and that you must ask any questions you want before you start the questionnaire. You will be told that there is no time limit.

■ The administrator will check that you have a pencil or a biro, a question booklet and an answer sheet. If a computer is being used, it will be checked to see that it is working properly. (If you are using a computer, you may well be completing the questionnaire by yourself. This is because it is too expensive to have a room full of computers that are used just for testing.)

■ You will be asked to record your name and date on the answer paper. The instructions will be read out on the first page of the question booklet and you will be asked if you have any questions.

■ The instructions will normally include the following points:
  - How to fill in your answers on the answer paper.
  - There are no 'right' or 'wrong' answers, and to choose an answer which best reflects what you are like.
  - Not to spend too long on any one question and to give the first answer that comes to you.
  - You should answer all the questions and be careful not to get out of sequence.
  - Not to resort to the 'middle', 'maybe' or '?' response if you can avoid it (if the questionnaire includes this option).
  - To be as honest as you can and to give the answers that illustrate what you are really like.

■ The administrator may walk around the room from time to time to make sure that people are recording their answers in the correct place on the answer paper.

■ When everybody has finished, the question booklets and answer papers will be collected. You will be thanked for attending the assessment session and the administrator will explain what will happen to the results.

Questionnaire strategies

As with any sort of assessment, you should make sure that you arrive at the assessment session at least 15 minutes before it is due to begin, and that you have had a good night's sleep. If you wear reading glasses or a hearing aid, make sure that you bring them with you. Also, if you find it difficult to go for a number of hours without something to eat or drink, bring some refreshments with you. There is usually a break halfway through the session when you will have an opportunity to consume your snack or visit the washroom.

With regard to answering the questions, by far the best advice is to be as honest as you can. There are a number of good reasons for this:

- There will be many questions relating to specific personality characteristics or dimensions. If you give the answer you think is likely to do you the most good, but which is actually unlike you, you will have to do this with all the subsequent questions. It is difficult to be consistent in this way when you have to recognise particular questions out of as many as 200.
- As explained in Chapter 2, the questionnaire may contain special scales to determine whether your answers are too good to be true, or if you are only giving 'socially desirable' responses.
- If you emphasise one thing it might well be at the expense of another, perhaps even more important, aspect of your personality.
- You don't know what the ideal profile for the job might be. You might actually have the 'right' sort of personality already.
- You may answer very consistently and spot all the special questions and end up with a job to which you are not suited. This may cause you a great deal of stress and ultimately be somewhat embarrassing.

However, you can still present yourself in the best possible light. The five tips that follow are designed to maximise your chances of coming across as a strong and well-balanced personality.

Five hot tips

1. **Find out as much as you can about yourself.** To help you do this, refer to the Self-Discovery Exercise in Chapter 1. You will also find the Mind Style Questionnaire in Chapter 5 one of the best ways of finding out what a personality questionnaire is likely to say about you. Remember that questionnaires are concerned with how much self-insight you have. They are, in effect, just asking you a series of questions about yourself, so become an expert on your own personality. A final tip is to link up to the Internet and to have a go at some of the practice material that is available. Try the Saville & Holdsworth and ASE sites at www.shlgroup.com and www.ase-solutions.co.uk, respectively. Typing words like 'personality', 'psychology tests' or 'psychometrics' into a Web search engine should also produce more places for you to visit.

2. **You must be positive.** The mistake that many people make when they are asked to describe themselves honestly is that they are either far too hard on themselves or they are completely unrealistic. The best thing to do is to think of yourself on a good day at work, or on a good day in your last job, and just imagine how you would describe yourself to a potential employer. If you haven't had a job, try to think how you would describe yourself to your best friend.

3. **Don't 'argue' with the questions.** Another classic mistake is to over-analyse the questions to such an

extent that you don't know what is being asked. For example, these are the thoughts you might have in response to the question 'Do you like going to parties?': What sort of a party is it? Is it one where I know all the people? Is it a party with music or dancing? Is it a night-time or daytime party? Is it fancy dress? Clearly, the list could go on, but the more you think about it the harder it becomes to answer. For questions of this type, it is best simply to give your first 'gut' reaction.

4. **'Try to answer as if you were like everyone else is supposed to be'.** This piece of advice was given by William Whyte in the book *The Organisation Man*. Whyte, who wrote his book for aspiring (male) business executives, also went on to give the following, more detailed observations:

Repeat to yourself:

a) I loved my father and my mother, but my father a little bit more.
b) I like things pretty well the way they are.
c) I never worry much about anything.
d) I don't care for books or music much.
e) I love my wife and children.
f) I don't let them get in the way of my company work.

Nowadays, this would be seen as the classic prescription for a well-adjusted, conservative, anxiety-free, extroverted and competitive worker for a large multinational company. However, do note that this may not be the perfect profile for many other jobs.

5. **Research the job or position for which you are applying.** If, in the words of the song, you are really going to 'accentuate the positive and eliminate the negative', make sure that you have a very good idea of

the profile for the job. You may get some clues from the description of the job in the advertisement, if that is where you learnt about it, or from any information that was sent to you prior to the test session. Also, ask organisations to send you any corporate literature they produce, or anything which gives details of the business and the people who work for it – eg, the company annual report. They may even be kind enough to send you a practice version of the personality questionnaire itself – see the example that follows.

The real trick to producing an effective performance is to be yourself. Unless you are very clever and have an exceptional memory, it is extremely difficult to distort systematically the results of a personality questionnaire. Also, bear in mind that you will have to live up to your 'improved' personality in the interview.

OPQ® practice questionnaire

An Introduction to

Personality Questionnaires

Questionnaires are used by employers and careers advisors to help gain a picture of how people match different jobs. This leaflet is designed to help you understand more about questionnaires and help you prepare for completing them.

Personality questionnaires, (or inventories), are concerned with people's typical or preferred ways of behaving, such as, the way they relate to others, or the way they approach and solve problems. The benefit of a questionnaire is that the same carefully designed and fully researched questions are asked of all people and their answers are captured and interpreted in a fair, consistent and objective way.

Questionnaires typically explore the broad range of personality characteristics which are generally relevant to the world of work. They are often used by organisations where information is required about an individual, for example, in development, selection or counselling. When questionnaires are used with other methods of assessment they can help to ensure a more thorough exploration of how well a person is suited to a particular job.

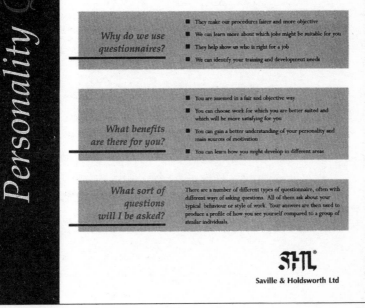

Why do we use questionnaires?
- They make our procedures fairer and more objective
- We can learn more about which jobs might be suitable for you
- They help show us who is right for a job
- We can identify your training and development needs

What benefits are there for you?
- You are assessed in a fair and objective way
- You can choose work for which you are better suited and which will be more satisfying for you
- You can gain a better understanding of your personality and main sources of motivation
- You can learn how you might develop in different areas

What sort of questions will I be asked?
There are a number of different types of questionnaire, often with different ways of asking questions. All of them ask about your typical behaviour or style of work. Your answers are then used to produce a profile of how you see yourself compared to a group of similar individuals.

SHL®
Saville & Holdsworth Ltd

Here are some examples of the types of questions that might be asked.

1 Rating Statements

In this example you are asked to rate yourself on a number of phrases or statements. After reading each statement mark your answer according to the following rules:

Fill in circle 1	If you strongly disagree with the statement
Fill in circle 2	If you disagree with the statement
Fill in circle 3	If you are unsure
Fill in circle 4	If you agree with the statement
Fill in circle 5	If you strongly agree with the statement

The first statement has already been completed for you. The person has agreed that 'I enjoy meeting new people' is an accurate description of him/herself.

Now try questions 2 to 6 for yourself by completely filling in the circle that is most true for you.

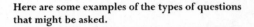

	Strongly disagree	Disagree	Unsure	Agree	Strongly agree
1 I enjoy meeting new people	①	②	③	●	⑤
2 I like helping people	①	②	③	④	⑤
3 I sometimes make mistakes	①	②	③	④	⑤
4 I don't mind taking risks	①	②	③	④	⑤
5 I'm easily disappointed	①	②	③	④	⑤
6 I enjoy repairing things	①	②	③	④	⑤

2   Making Choices

In this example you are given a block of four statements: A, B, C and D. Your task is to choose the statement which you think is most true or typical of you in your everyday behaviour and then choose the one which is least true or typical of you. Indicate your choices by filling in the appropriate circle in the row marked 'M' (for Most) and in the next row 'L' (for Least).

The first block has been completed for you. The person has chosen, 'Enjoys organising people' as most true (or typical) and "Seeks variety" as being least true (or typical) of him/herself. Now try questions ?, 3 and 4 yourself.

I am the sort of person who.......

1   A   Has a wide circle of friends
     B   Enjoys organising people
     C   Relaxes easily
     D   Seeks variety

2   A   Helps people with their problems
     B   Develops new approaches
     C   Has lots of energy
     D   Enjoys social activities

3   A   Has lots of new ideas
     B   Feels calm
     C   Likes to understand things
     D   Is easy to get on with

4   A   Enjoys organising events
     B   Sometimes gets angry
     C   Is talkative
     D   Resolves conflicts at work

Personality

How do I complete a questionnaire ?

Often personality questionnaires are completed using paper and pencil. Typically you will be asked to fill in circles to indicate your answers as in the examples here. Sometimes however computers are used. In this situation you won't need to know how to operate a computer. Everything you have to do will be explained at the session and you will be given a chance to practise using the computer and ask questions before you start. Whether you use paper and pencil or a computer you will be asked the same kinds of question.

Final points about personality questionnaires

- The questions are concerned with how you typically behave at work. Thinking about a typical work situation may help you answer. If you have no formal work experience, think about how you behave in similar situations such as voluntary work, school, college or when doing other tasks, for example, housework and hobbies.

- Although there is no time limit, you should work quickly rather than pondering at length over any one question. This helps you give your most natural answer, the one which best reflects how you are.

- Make sure you answer all the questions.

- People who try to guess what is wanted are often incorrect and may give an impression of themselves which doesn't fit in with other information. Many questionnaires contain questions which help to check whether someone is describing themselves honestly and consistently, so try to be as accurate as possible when answering the questions.

- We may want to discuss your results with you. If you are offered this opportunity use it to find out as much about yourself as you can. This may be helpful to you in understanding yourself and your strengths and limitations better.

- The questionnaire is about your personality style, that is, the way you go about things. It is not about ability and there are no right or wrong answers. Just answer as you are.

- Don't worry if some questions do not seem relevant. We will be focusing on those areas most relevant to your situation.

- The results will typically form only part of an assessment and will be interpreted alongside other information about you.

- We will respect the confidentiality of your results.

Key points

- Personality questionnaires are used in conjunction with other tests.
- Questionnaire booklets contain guidance on how to answer the questions.
- All personality questionnaires are administered by trained staff. If you don't know what do do, *ask*.
- Don't try to 'second guess' the test designer. Give the first answer that comes to you.
- Watch out for questions that invite you to exaggerate your virtues. Remember that questionnaires can contain questions that detect 'impression management'.
- Know yourself thoroughly and follow the series of tips given in this chapter.

5

The Mind Style Questionnaire

This chapter contains a complete practice personality questionnaire – the Mind Style Questionnaire (MSQ). The MSQ is a self-report, 'Big Five' measure, constructed using the latest research on personality measurement. It is relatively short in that it contains only 88 questions. However, this is still longer than the two most popular quick questionnaires available in the UK (see Chapter 7).

This is not the place to explain the scoring system in detail, but the MSQ contains a number of features that help to make your answers more positive and to make the results more accurate. For example, each question measures only one aspect of your personality, so saying 'No', or in fact 'False', does *not* mean that you score at the opposite end of a dimension – eg, disagreeing with an 'extroverted' question does not automatically make you 'introverted'.

The other point to bear in mind when you work out your results is that most people are not at the extremes of each dimension, but towards the middle. Statistically, you would expect to find about 40 per cent in the 'average' range, with the remaining 60 per cent split between the two ends of a dimension – eg, 20 per cent highly, and 10 per cent very highly extroverted; and 20 per cent highly, and 10 per cent very highly introverted. Furthermore, personality is neither 'good' nor 'bad'. It does not work in such a simple way. Each personality characteristic is a mixture of features that may or may not be useful, but this is only apparent when you actually apply your personality to work, to relationships, to education, or whatever.

Completing the questionnaire

The Mind Style Questionnaire is designed to find out what you are like as a person. It asks you about the way in which you react in different situations and how you deal with other people.

As with any personality questionnaire, there are no 'right' or 'wrong' answers; the idea is that you just say what is most like you. This can be difficult at times, but the more honest you are, the more accurate and useful the results will be.

You fill in your answers by putting a tick in the appropriate box. – eg:

	True	False
A. I like to work by myself.	☐	✓
B. I enjoy games of skill.	☐	✓
C. People trust my judgement.	✓	☐

When you answer the questions, bear the following points in mind:

1. Don't spend too long thinking about each question, just give the first answer that comes into your head.
2. Make sure that you answer *all* the questions. If you change your mind about an answer, cross it out clearly and put a tick in the other box.
3. Even if a question does not seem entirely relevant, give the answer you consider would be most like you.

4. There is no time limit, but try to complete the questionnaire as quickly as you can.
5. *Don't look at the scoring key until you have done the questionnaire!*

Start when you are ready

		True	False
1.	I can easily talk to people about how I feel.	☐	☐
2.	If something goes wrong it preys on my mind.	☐	☐
3.	I like things to be neat and tidy.	☐	☐
4.	I'm good at listening to other people's problems.	☐	☐
5.	I tend to use tried and tested methods.	☐	☐
6.	I like to have plenty of time to myself.	☐	☐
7.	If people are rude to me I just shrug it off.	☐	☐
8.	I can work even when things are disorganised.	☐	☐
9.	I'm a competitive person.	☐	☐
10.	I like to have lots of variety in what I do.	☐	☐
11.	I enjoy talking to people at social gatherings.	☐	☐
12.	I always feel hurt if someone criticises me.	☐	☐
13.	I have a systematic way of doing most things.	☐	☐
14.	I tend to trust other people.	☐	☐
15.	I am a practical-minded sort of person.	☐	☐
16.	I never tell 'white' lies.	☐	☐
17.	I'm more of a listener than a talker.	☐	☐
18.	I seldom suffer from feelings of stress.	☐	☐
19.	It's better to get a job done than aim for perfection.	☐	☐
20.	I like to be in charge of other people.	☐	☐
21.	I like coming up with new ideas.	☐	☐
22.	I am happy to make speeches in public.	☐	☐
23.	Sometimes little things really upset me.	☐	☐
24.	I always tell people exactly what I think.	☐	☐
25.	I like to have a daily routine.	☐	☐

		True	**False**
26.	People often thank me for my support.	☐	☐
27.	I like to work within the rules.	☐	☐
28.	I feel uneasy if I'm the centre of attention.	☐	☐
29.	I am cool-headed when under pressure.	☐	☐
30.	I never worry about a bit of untidyness.	☐	☐
31.	I often lose my patience with other people.	☐	☐
32.	None of my close friends has ever upset me.	☐	☐
33.	I like to know how things work.	☐	☐
34.	I enjoy socialising with large groups of people.	☐	☐
35.	After a hard day I find it difficult to unwind.	☐	☐
36.	If I say I will do something, I always do it.	☐	☐
37.	I worry when people are unhappy.	☐	☐
38.	People describe me as having good common sense.	☐	☐
39.	I prefer to talk to people on a one-to-one basis.	☐	☐
40.	I can't remember ever being late for an appointment.	☐	☐
41.	I keep going whatever happens.	☐	☐
42.	Sometimes you have to break 'the rules'.	☐	☐
43.	I'm good at getting people to do things.	☐	☐
44.	My ideas are not always practical.	☐	☐
45.	I like it when people call in unannounced.	☐	☐
46.	I always get keyed up before important events.	☐	☐
47.	I don't leave jobs unfinished.	☐	☐
48.	I always keep other people's secrets.	☐	☐
49.	I find it easy to put myself in someone else's position.	☐	☐
50.	I'm a down-to-earth sort of person.	☐	☐
51.	I'm happy sitting at home reading a book.	☐	☐
52.	I take a relaxed view about most things.	☐	☐
53.	I like to react to things on the spur of the moment.	☐	☐
54.	I always get what I want from people.	☐	☐

		True	False
55.	I like to think of new ways of doing things.	☐	☐
56.	I'm happy to see people, whatever the circumstances.	☐	☐
57.	I like playing noisy competitive games.	☐	☐
58.	I don't like unexpected responsibilities.	☐	☐
59.	I often find myself clearing up other people's mess.	☐	☐
60.	I'm good at detecting 'uncomfortable' atmospheres.	☐	☐
61.	I tend to 'live and let live'.	☐	☐
62.	If I'm doing something I don't like to be interrupted.	☐	☐
63.	I don't let things get on top of me.	☐	☐
64.	I never worry if I make a mistake.	☐	☐
65.	I often lose track of time.	☐	☐
66.	I'm a 'bad loser' at games.	☐	☐
67.	People sometimes say that my 'head is in the clouds'.	☐	☐
68.	I often act on impulse.	☐	☐
69.	I tend to be a cautious person.	☐	☐
70.	I never leave things to the last minute.	☐	☐
71.	People often comment on how patient I am.	☐	☐
72.	I've never been deliberately rude to anyone.	☐	☐
73.	I don't usually have extreme views on things.	☐	☐
74.	I need quiet to work effectively.	☐	☐
75.	I am good at dealing with difficult people.	☐	☐
76.	I take each day as it comes.	☐	☐
77.	I like to challenge people and make them think.	☐	☐
78.	I am curious about most things.	☐	☐
79.	I often say things without thinking about them.	☐	☐
80.	Sometimes I feel guilty even if I haven't done anything.	☐	☐
81.	I can be something of a perfectionist.	☐	☐

	True	False
82. I tend to avoid confrontations.	☐	☐
83. I like to deal with factual information.	☐	☐
84. I have a small number of really good friends.	☐	☐
85. I respond well in any sort of crisis.	☐	☐
86. I often lose things.	☐	☐
87. I don't back down in an argument.	☐	☐
88. People see me as an 'ideas' person.	☐	☐

End of questionnaire

✓ *Check that you have ticked a box for each question.*

Scoring the questionnaire

To score the questionnaire you need to calculate the total scores for the five personality dimensions. Each scale has two ends, so there are ten simple calculations to complete. For example, the first dimension indicates whether you are predominantly extroverted or introverted, or a combination of both.

When you start the scoring, you will see that all the extroverted questions have negative (–) scores, and all the introverted questions have positive scores (+). (The fact that some things are negative and other things are positive does *not* mean that certain answers are better than others; it is just a way of calculating the balance of extroversion against introversion).

To make the calculation, you simply add up all the negative extroverted scores, add up all the positive introverted scores, and then add the two numbers together – eg:

Extroverted total	=	–10	Introverted total	= + 6
Overall total	=	–4 (ie: –10 plus + 6)		

or:

Extroverted total	=	–5	Introverted total	= + 12
Overall total	=	+7 (ie: –5 plus + 12)		

The calculations for the other four dimensions are done in exactly the same way. The tables that follow will help you to work out your five overall totals.

Step 1

In each of the tables, put a tick by the question numbers to which you answered 'True'. Ignore all those questions to which you answered 'False'. When you have ticked all the questions to which you answered True for both aspects of a dimension, add up the appropriate numbers in the two score columns, noting that some questions score more than others. Finally, add the two totals together, negative to positive, to get your overall score for the dimension. (It is possible to score 0, which indicates that you are in the middle of a dimension.)

Dimension 1

	Extroverted				Introverted	
Question	✓	Score		Question	✓	Score
1		−1		6		+2
11		−2		17		+2
22		−2		28		+2
34		−2		39		+1
45		−1		51		+1
57		−1		62		+1
68		−1		74		+1
79		−2		84		+2
	Total =				Total =	

Overall total = extroverted + introverted
Overall total = ...

Dimension 2

Tough minded				Tender minded		
Question	✓	Score		Question	✓	Score
9		−1		4		+2
20		−2		14		+1
31		−1		26		+1
43		−1		37		+2
54		−2		49		+2
66		−2		60		+1
77		−1		71		+2
87		−2		82		+1
	Total =				Total =	

Overall total = Tough minded + Tender minded
Overall total = ...

Dimension 3

Conforming				Creative		
Question	✓	Score		Question	✓	Score
5		−2		10		+1
15		−1		21		+2
27		−2		33		+1
38		−2		44		+1
50		−1		55		+2
61		−1		67		+2
73		−2		78		+1
83		−1		88		+2
	Total =				Total =	

Overall total = Conforming + Creative
Overall total = ...

Dimension 4

High structure				Low structure		
Question	✓	Score		Question	✓	Score
3		−2		8		+2
13		−2		19		+1
25		−1		30		+2
36		−1		42		+1
47		−1		53		+2
59		−2		65		+1
70		−1		76		+1
81		−2		86		+2
	Total =				Total =	

Overall total = High structure + Low structure
Overall total = ...

Dimension 5

Confident				Emotional		
Question	✓	Score		Question	✓	Score
7		−2		2		+2
18		−2		12		+1
29		−1		23		+2
41		−1		35		+1
52		−1		46		+2
63		−2		58		+1
75		−2		69		+1
85		−1		80		+2
	Total =				Total =	

Overall total = Confident + Emotional
Overall total = ...

Step 2

Complete the table below to work out your impression control score:

Impression control

Question	✓	Score
16		+2
24		+2
32		+1
40		+1
48		+2
56		+1
64		+2
72		+1
	Total =	

Overall total = Impression control
Overall total = ...

Step 3

You should now have six overall totals, five for the personality dimensions and one for impression control.

Now you need to scale your totals. You do this by using the Scaling Table that follows. For example, you will see that if your total score on Dimension 1 is –9, it becomes –5; if it is +4, it becomes +2. Do this for each of your totals and put the results in the Summary Table.

Note: A total score of (0) stays at (0); and your impression control score will always be positive (+).

Scaling Table

A score of:	becomes:	A score of:	becomes:
−12	−6	+12	+6
−11	−6	+11	+6
−10	−5	+10	+5
−9	−5	+9	+5
−8	−4	+8	+4
−7	−4	+7	+4
−6	−3	+6	+3
−5	−3	+5	+3
−4	−2	+4	+2
−3	−2	+3	+2
−2	−1	+2	+1
−1	−1	+1	+1

Summary Table

Dimension 1 (Extroverted ⇔ Introverted)	= ....
Dimension 2 (Tough minded ⇔ Tender minded)	= ....
Dimension 3 (Conforming ⇔ Creative)	= ....
Dimension 4 (High structure ⇔ Low structure)	= ....
Dimension 5 (Confident ⇔ Emotional)	= ....
Impression control	= ....

Step 4

Plot your results on the MSQ Summary Chart. You do this by filling in the little square that represents your overall (scaled) total for each dimension and for Impression Control. If you like, you can also fill in one square before and one square after, each of your scores. This illustrates the variability of your scores as there is always a small amount of 'error' when your measure anything, including personality. You should end up with a chart that looks similar to the example in Chapter 3 (page 45).

MSQ Summary Chart

← – scores	6	5	4	3	2	1	0	1	2	3	4	5	6	+ scores ➡
Extroverted											²			Introverted
Tough minded												′		Tender minded
Conforming			♭											Creative
High structure			∗											Low structure
Confident								⸌						Emotional
Impression control						⸆								

Step 5

Determine whether each of your scores is 'average', 'high' or 'very high'.

Average. If you score between –2 and +2 (inclusive), you will show characteristics from each end of the dimension, – eg, extroverted *and* introverted, depending on the circumstances in which you find yourself.

High. If you score between –3 and –5 (inclusive), or between +3 and +5 (inclusive), you will have a definite tendency to show the characteristics described for the appropriate end of the dimension – eg, extroverted *or* introverted a good deal of the time.

Very High. If your score is –6 or +6, you will show the extremes of the appropriate dimension – eg, you will be *predominantly* extroverted or introverted.

If you want to be very precise about your scores, you should take into account the 'error' mentioned earlier. In reality, this means that your score on each dimension could be one unit bigger or smaller. For example, if your score on the first dimension is +3, it actually ranges from +2 to +4. This could make a difference to the interpretation as you may fall between two of the above categories – eg, you may actually be average to high, or high to very high on a particular dimension.

It is important to realise that your scores relate to you as an individual. On the basis of this questionnaire, you may be more extroverted than you are introverted, but no attempt has been made to compare you precisely with the rest of the population. This *would* happen if you were being selected for a job. In fact, you might well be compared with a representative sample of people who already do the job, who in turn might be more extroverted than the general population. So, for example, an employer might actually be looking for 'high' or 'very high' scores, or, under different circumstances, only for 'average' scores. It depends on the requirements for a particular job.

Step 6

Interpreting your results

Look at the descriptions that follow to find out about your personality profile:

Dimension 1: Extroverted ⇔ Introverted

Extroverted people are open, talkative, expressive and lively. They enjoy other people's attention and like social gatherings. They are good at meeting people and dealing with strangers, and are generally energetic, active and enjoy taking risks. However, they can act on impulse and may not always think through the consequences of their actions. This can mean that they 'rush in where angels fear to tread'. Sometimes such unplanned actions can be seen as irresponsible.

In a work context, extroverts prefer to work with people, usually in teams or groups. They do not like doing jobs by themselves, and prefer to seek out other people's views and to collaborate jointly on projects. Highly extroverted people may appear to be very outspoken and will actively (and sometimes very assertively) put their point of view across. This can be an advantage in situations where persuasive skills are required – eg, in selling situations.

Introverted people are quiet and reserved. They like to keep themselves to themselves, and are content with their own thoughts and feelings. They do not need the company of other people (as an extrovert would), and are unlikely to seek out actively and attend social gatherings. They do not usually act in an impulsive way, and are more likely to think things through carefully before they do them. The theme is generally one of stability and considered decision making.

At work, introverted people may be seen as shy, restrained and rather distant, and this can mean that they are sometimes overlooked. However, they are usually good at working by themselves, or in small groups, and this is an important factor in many jobs. In those situations where an introverted person has a good command of the relevant information or the appropriate experience, he can appear to be just as confident as the extrovert.

Dimension 2: Tough minded ⇔ Tender minded

Tough-minded people are assertive and achievement orientated. They tend to focus on the task at hand and can appear at times to be insensitive. Their view is that people are responsible for their own actions. Thus, the very tough-minded person is likely to be irritated if he has to deal with other people's problems, and may well appear rather intolerant.

In the work context, the mentality is one of winning, even if this is at the expense of someone else. This is a sign of a strong competitive streak, and of a determined and single-minded approach to the job. The same single-mindedness is also mirrored in social and leisure activities: tough-minded people like to win and are very poor losers. Whatever they do, they like to be 'in charge' and to seek to influence and control others. They tend to put their point of view over confidently and enjoy being the centre of attention.

Tender-minded people are warm, caring and considerate. They are concerned for those around them and how they feel. Other people see them as friendly and helpful, and as respecting different points of view. This empathy with other people is generally coupled with a sharing, co-operative approach to life. However, the problem with such a 'benevolent' personality is that other people may take advantage of it. This is reinforced by the fact that tender-minded people are not overtly ambitious, do not seek social prominence, and tend to keep out of the spotlight: it is an easy-going, 'take life as it comes' attitude.

At work, tender-minded people are viewed as being sensitive

and approachable. As such, they tend to take on other people's problems, sometimes at the expense of their own well-being. They also dislike conflict and are uncomfortable giving orders to other people. This means that they are not usually natural leaders, but may do well in supportive and socially sensitive roles.

Dimension 3: Conforming ⇔ Creative

Conforming people are conservative, down to earth and moderate. They like to deal with what they know, and to solve problems using tried and tested methods. This is a pragmatic, low-risk approach to life, frequently characterised by a high degree of self-discipline. As such, conforming people would not describe themselves as being particularly creative. However, they are usually skilled at adapting existing methods. This is not to be dismissed lightly, as those who build on ideas in a practical way usually reap the benefits.

At work, conforming people tend to defend the established way of doing things. They value integrity and like to provide a good example for others to follow. However, this protection of the status quo is often seen as a resistance to new ideas and to change. In extreme circumstances, this may also be viewed as a rejection of the need to debate alternative ways of working. Thus, the conforming person strives to avoid risk and favours stability. In consequence, work environments that do not change, have well-established rules and an understood routine, will tend to be the most attractive. This generally means larger rather than smaller organisations.

Creative people are open-minded individuals who like to experiment with unconventional ways of doing things. They are always on the lookout for a new method or a way of getting round the rules. They like to come up with numerous ideas and they enjoy change. This can mean that they are resistant to tradition and will tend to fight against what may be perfectly good ways of solving problems. As the creative solution is not always very practical, creative people will sometimes be described as having their 'heads stuck in the clouds'.

At work, creative people tend to embrace new opportunities and promote innovative methods. Other people will see them as enthusiasts, but at times as not very reliable or consistent. This desire to be different can lead to other sorts of problems, and highly creative people are unlikely to be placed in charge of teams. The reason for the latter is that they are better at generating ideas for other people to work on, rather than being able to take command of operations. Indeed, left to their own devices, creative people would probably take risks that would lead to real business problems or, in the worst case, failure.

Dimension 4: High structure ⇔ Low structure

High structure people take a precise, controlled and formal approach to their life and work. They are sensitive to detail and like things to be done on time. This is frequently a sign of great self-control and restraint and also of a marked intolerance to clutter and mess. At times, the control the high-structure person brings to tasks can be seen by others as obsessive. This perfectionist approach can also cause problems if tasks have to be completed within very tight time deadlines.

At work, high-structure people will appear organised and in control. Indeed, they may even be admired by those who are less tidy and find organising their work a chore. However, they may also be quite difficult to deal with as they demand very high standards from other people.

High-structure people in the workplace usually have an extremely tidy desk, with their papers in precise heaps and their writing instruments gathered together in a container. They always clear their papers away at the end of the day.

Low-structure people are not detail conscious and can be quite casual about the way in which they do things. They are tolerant of other people's methods and take an informal approach to daily life. They are not concerned by clutter and disorganisation, and can happily work in chaotic surroundings (which a high-structure person would find extremely uncomfortable). A low-structure approach is also characterised by an enthusiasm for starting things off, but with a rapid loss of interest if a project takes longer than expected. In addition, there is a tendency to become bored easily and to suffer a degree of absent-mindedness – eg, losing things and being late for appointments.

At work, low-structure people are good at getting things started but need to be complemented by more organised colleagues if jobs are to be done precisely. For example, they are unlikely to get things done on time without copious reminders. However, in contrast to the high-structure person, they do not suffer from an overly perfectionist style, which can also be a real brake to progress.

Dimension 5: Confident ⇔ emotional

Confident people are relaxed, assertive individuals. They know their own minds and are comfortable with themselves. Their approach is usually characterised by an optimistic and positive view of the world. They can take criticism and do not spend time worrying about what other people think about them. The highly confident person is unlikely to suffer from stress or to be troubled by most things. As a result, other people may well describe them as being 'thick-skinned'. This supreme lack of concern can make the very confident person appear to be somewhat blasé.

At work, confident people stand their ground and defend their view of how things should be done. They will be seen by others as 'cool headed', even when they are severely provoked. However, while these can be desirable qualities, confident people can often be difficult to motivate as they tend not to react to criticism or censure. Yet practically, they are unlikely to 'go to pieces' in stressful situations and can cope well with pressure.

Emotional people are frequently rather tense and anxious. They worry about what other people think and find it difficult to ignore what is going on around them. In many situations, an emotional person will fret, even over small problems. This worrying can become acute, especially before important events. At times, matters are made even worse by the fact that emotional people often find it difficult to relax or to 'switch off'.

At work, emotional people will be sensitive to criticism and will try very hard therefore not to make mistakes. They tend to plan things to reduce the chance of problems occurring. As such, they can act as useful counterweights to their overly confident work colleagues. However, unlike the confident person, if things go really wrong, the emotional person may well panic. Sometimes the sense that things are out of control can bring the emotional person close to tears.

Impression control

The impression control scale is designed to find out whether you have a tendency to present yourself in an overly positive manner. The questions ask about facts that the vast majority of people, if they are honest with themselves, rate as being 'True'. For example, we have all told 'white lies' at one time or another; very few people *always* say exactly what they think; your close friends are bound to have upset or annoyed you at some time; we have all been late for an appointment; told someone's secret to another; pretended to be out when we didn't want to see someone; worried over a mistake; and have been driven (even mildly) to rudeness on occasions.

If you have a total score of over four, you are probably not being completely honest with yourself. In this case, the best thing to do is to complete the questionnaire again. This time ignore what you feel are the most 'socially desirable' answers and reflect on what you are really like.

Some things to remember

The Mind Style Questionnaire may have confirmed what you know about yourself or contained a number of surprises. If you were surprised or discovered something with which you disagree, just bear in mind that it gives a very broad view of your personality. Each of the dimensions could quite easily be broken down into many smaller categories. If this had been done, some of the finer points of your personality would have emerged. Also, remember that you did the questionnaire by yourself and that it was not administered or controlled by a psychologist. This would most definitely be the case if you completed a questionnaire as part of the selection process for a job. The results would also have been compared with a representative sample of other people – ie, an appropriate normative group.

Strictly speaking, if you want a really accurate view of your personality, you need to complete a number of questionnaires under carefully controlled conditions. This can be arranged and if you are interested, you could contact a professional psychologist (look in *Yellow Pages*) or a local careers organisation. They will be able to give you a detailed assessment of your personality, which is invaluable in the search for a suitable career or when applying for a job. After all, it is useful to know what an employer is likely to discover about you. It is also the case that if you realise what you are like, you can try to change certain aspects of your personality if you wish. Although you cannot change your basic personality, you can develop appropriate coping mechanisms.

For example, you can train yourself to be more adaptable or to be more organised and structured. Some of these techniques are described in the next chapter.

Finally, you might like to consider the observation made by the German psychologist, Angleitner. He likened the results of personality questionnaires to classifying living things as animals or plants. Although it is an interesting analogy, to be more accurate it is more like classifying animals as either mammals, birds, fish, insects, amphibians or reptiles. The point is that these classifications contain creatures with very different characteristics. For example, both humans *and* whales are mammals, but there is something of a difference between us! So while personality questionnaires do help to classify our behaviour, even those of us who have 'identical' profiles will still show all sorts of individual differences.

Key points

- The Mind Style Questionnaire describes your personality using five dimensions.
- The interpretations describe how you are likely to behave in a variety of situations.
- Some aspects of your personality cannot be measured by this questionnaire.
- To obtain a really accurate picture of your personality, you need to complete a number of questionnaires.

6

The Personality Toolkit

These days most people are too busy getting on with the everyday business of living to stop and assess what they really want. However, it is important to reflect occasionally on what we want to achieve and how we are going to get there. Part of this process involves looking at our own thoughts and feelings, values and attitudes, and critically, at what motivates us to do things.

If you have completed the Mind Style Questionnaire you will have discovered a few things about your personality. Hopefully, you will feel that the results are reasonably accurate. But what is the next step? I mentioned earlier that although a person's personality may change throughout his life, it is a gradual process. It appears to be stable because we do not switch radically from one personality to another. However, while your basic personality may be stable, you can still change your approach to situations, or even change your way of responding towards other people, at a *practical* level. Naturally, the first step is to find out, in a reasonably objective way, what you are like.

In the pages that follow we will look at where you want to get to in your working life and what you can do to alter your pattern of behaviour. At this point you might ask, why bother? Indeed, if you are happy with your personality, this is a perfectly sensible question. However, there are few people who would not benefit from a greater insight into what makes them the way they are, and from practical ways of coping with what they are like. The issue is really one of self-development and of getting the most out of work, relationships, education and the future.

Some people feel that playing about with their personality is frightening. However, the issue is not one of changing someone's basic personality, but of helping them to modify the behaviour that springs *from* a particular personality. Far from being a dubious activity, this is a natural thing to do, as studies have shown that between adulthood and middle-age, 69 per cent of people actually change their ratings of their own personality. To look at it another way, during this period of about 20 years, the majority of people develop new ways of using their personality. This does not mean that people are running around acting out what they would like to be, rather that there are ways of comfortably changing their behaviour, and hence of other people's perceptions of them – an important factor when it comes to being selected for a job or for forming any sort of satisfying relationship.

How people change

The way in which you present yourself is something over which you have control, yet some people will have more control than others. However, irrespective of the sort of person you are, you can choose to change yourself or to adapt to the situation in which you find yourself. The effect of changing depends on how much you want to change and the speed at which you want to do it. You should bear in mind that for most people rapid change is quite stressful and that while we can all 'act' a part for a short time, it requires a great deal of energy to do it for a long period. Thus, the secret is to incorporate changes in your behaviour that complement or boost the changes you could make naturally, with a little effort. In a work context, this can mean adopting a style that is different from your 'off-duty' personality. Those who think this sounds artificial should consider the various activities we do everyday. Is there a single 'social' situation when we are not trying to present ourselves in a particular, usually favourable, light?

We are all consciously, or unconsciously, trying to influence other people. It may be on special occasions, like an interview or a business meeting, or more generally when we are trying to present an image of ourselves to our friends, partners or acquaintances. So whether you like it or not, you do it all the time, and in many instances without even having to think about it. Furthermore, most people use the same four techniques, regardless of their personality, for impressing other people. These techniques are:

- **Behaviour matching.** This is when we mirror another person's behaviour. For example, if someone tells us something personal, we tend to respond with some personal information of our own.
- **Conformity.** We adopt the correct behaviour for the situation. For example, there are differences between the way in which you would act at a party and at an employment interview.
- **Appreciation.** A little flattery can go a long way, and we try to be actively interested in what someone has achieved or in the information he discloses about himself.
- **Consistency.** We act in a predictable way. For example, if we want to be taken seriously we do not support a person one moment and attack them the next. That is because we all know that inconsistency is usually taken as a sign of weakness.

Clearly, these are not the only behavioural techniques you can use to influence other people, but before we look at more we need to give our search a focus. This could be, for example, on developing personal relationships. However, since the subject of this book is personality and employment, the focus will be on self-development in a work context.

The first step in the process of self-development is to identify those features of work that you consider to be important. Once you have done this, you can decide on the aspects of your behaviour on which you would like to focus, remembering that there is much research to show that personal growth and development is directly related to job satisfaction. The following exercise is a good way of focusing on the important factors.

The ideal job exercise

In this exercise you write a description of your ideal job. This should include all those aspects that you feel are personally important or that you would like to develop. To help you begin, you might like to consider the work values that are important to you. For example:

- Do you like a structured working environment? *Do you value a well-defined job, conformity, security, predictability, and regular ways of doing things?*
- Do you want to achieve? *Do you like to be recognised and rewarded for what you do, and to feel a personal sense of achievement?*
- Do you want independence? *Is it important that you do not have someone 'breathing down your neck'? That you have freedom and flexibility in what you do? That you do not have to work regular 9 to 5 hours?*
- Do you want power? *Many people value power, but do you actually want to control other people and dictate what they do?*
- Do you want to be creative? *Is it important that you can use your imagination, or express yourself in a creative way? That you have many new tasks to do?*

- Do you want to help other people? *Are you driven by the need to put something back into society? To use your skills actively to help those who may not be able to help themselves?*
- Do you like to see a tangible end product? *It may be that you do not want to be one cog in a very large machine,but like to see a job through from beginning to end. If this is true, purely administrative jobs are probably not for you.*
- Do you want money? *Is it the thought of earning a large salary that motivates and drives you? Perhaps you don't mind what you do, as long as you get well rewarded.*
- Do you want to work with other people? *Some of us want to work alone or in one-to-one situations; others are only happy in large offices where they can talk to lots of other people.*

This is not an exhaustive list, but it should give you some ideas. You also need to consider the structure of your ideal organisation. What sort of goals does it have? Is it small or large? Does it have a complicated hierarchy or no hierarchy at all? What opportunities are there? Can you travel? Can you work in different countries?

Finally, what sorts of relationships do you want at work? How would the boss manage you? What would your work colleagues be like? What sorts of customers or clients would you like to deal with?

1. Now write your ideal description on a piece of paper. (If you want an example, part of a description is given at the end of this exercise.)
2. Look at your description and answer these four questions:

- Would you *really* be happy in this job?
- If not, what would you change about the job?
- Does your ideal job fit your personality, or MSQ results?
- If not, how would you change yourself?

The critical factor is the connection between how you are now and what the job demands. Where does your personality fit in? For example, are you really a shy person, but would like more responsibility? Do you tend to worry about things, but actually feel you want to take a few risks?

3. Summarise, on your paper, the four aspects of your behaviour on which you would like to work. A technique that might help you is to complete the following sentences:

■ My greatest wish is ...
■ I also want to ...
■ My greatest problem is ...
■ I also have problems with ...

Example ideal job

I would like to work in a relaxed environment where I was not always being told what to do. I am quite capable of working by myself and of setting my own targets. In fact, there are a number of parts of my job that I could do from home. It would be useful to be able to plan my week so that I could work at home, say, for two days and come into work for the other three. Having flexible hours is important because it means that you can fit work in to your life and vice versa.

The organisation would be small and friendly, and interested in everyone making the most of his potential. There would be an emphasis on training and keeping up-to-date with the latest technologies and techniques. Most of the work would be done in teams and they would be made up of the best people to do a particular job. My job in the team would be to provide the ideas and to get other people to think creatively. I would not be interested in being 'in charge' as I think that stifles innovation. Of course, we would have to work to time deadlines, but somebody else would do that.

I am an ambitious person and would like to be recognised as an expert in my field. I am not sure whether I would like to be a straightforward manager as that makes me think of great heaps of paperwork ...

The person who wrote the above description actually worked in a large, somewhat bureaucratic organisation. The points he focused on concerned flexibility, team membership, creativity and control. However, he realised that there was something of a conflict between his ambition and the sort of job he wanted. To fulfil his wish in real life it would be necessary to assume a higher profile. In reality, he was introverted and rather disorganised as an administrator. He also needed to take more responsibility for his own actions.

Ten ways to change

If you have completed the ideal job exercise, you should have identified some aspects of your behaviour that you want to explore. If you have not completed it, you should still find some of the techniques that follow of value. However, depending on how formal you want to be, there are six aspects of each 'problem' to examine. For example:

- What is the problem? *Being confident with new people and being able to talk to them in an open manner.*
- What does it affect? *My work and social activities.*
- Where does it happen? *At work with customers and at social events like parties.*
- When does it happen? *Most of the time. Although I do find it easy to talk to some people.*
- Why does it happen? *I am a shy person. I get embarrassed easily.*
- What can I do about it? *Learn ways of appearing, and of being, more extrovert.*

The example given is not at all unusual. So what can be done about it? The clue lies in the word 'extroverted', because what this person would like to be is less self-conscious and introspective, and more outgoing and sociable. What follows are guidelines on some of the ways of promoting this, and of other patterns of behaviour. The advice is centred on the five main personality dimensions used throughout this book:

1. 'I would like to be more assertive and socially skilled'

If you feel yourself to be more introverted than you would like you can address the 'problem' by concentrating on being more assertive and persuasive, and by developing your social skills. The question is really one of having more personal impact and of being comfortable interacting with other people.

Interestingly, when it comes to assertiveness, most people operate in one of three ways, or sometimes they switch at random between all three. So in those situations where you want to make a mark you either act submissively (a typically introverted approach), aggressively (which happens with some extroverts), or assertively. There is a difference between these responses in that assertive behaviour is about putting your point of view across in a positive way without 'steam-rollering' the other person; aggressive behaviour means standing up for your rights regardless of anyone else, and submissive behaviour means accepting what comes your way.

Most submissive people are self-effacing and tend to express what they think in an apologetic sort of manner. They use lots of qualifying phrases such as, 'If you have the time ...', 'Could you possibly ...' – and 'I'm sorry to bother you ...'. In addition, they tend to work around or avoid problems, rather than confront them. Thus, if you tend to be submissive and want to make a greater impact, consider using the following strategies:

- ■ Use more statements beginning with 'I' – eg, 'I think ...', 'I want ...', 'I feel ...'.
- ■ Try not to use qualifying statements – eg, 'Can you ...?' rather than 'I wonder if ...?'.

■ Actively ask other people what they think about things – eg, 'What do *you* think?'.
■ Suggest ways of fixing problems – eg, 'We could do …'.

These are also ways of being more persuasive (see Chapter 3). In addition, you will find that if you are more positive with other people, they will be more positive and interested in you. This will in turn make you feel more confident. Furthermore, in situations such as meetings or indeed just social gatherings, introverted people tend to be 'themselves' regardless of the social setting. This is actually a bad habit, because to fit into a social situation you actually have to behave in the appropriate way. I talked about this earlier when I highlighted the four main ways in which we tend to impress other people. It is also what distinguishes introverted people from extroverted people. Extroverts are always on the lookout for cues from other people as to how they should behave. In this way they are also quicker to respond to different situations and are more likely to start conversations. The trick for the introvert is to 'read' the situation more like an extrovert and to make the effort to match the mood of the situation. In a curious way, this actually means not letting your feelings dictate your behaviour. Thus, if you do not constantly worry about how you feel and whether or not you are enjoying a situation, you will actually feel more comfortable.

2. 'I would like to be more self-aware'

If you are a highly extroverted person you may need to become more self-aware and to consider your actions more thoroughly before you launch yourself into situations. This involves taking particular notice of your own behaviour, because it is only this sort of feedback that will help you to change. In particular, concentrate on the following sources:

- **Criticism.** This may sound like a strange thing on which to concentrate, but it is a useful source of direct personal feedback. So the next time that someone comments on your behaviour, hold on to the information and consider what it means. The chances are that if it is constructive feedback, they will have pinpointed an aspect of your behaviour that you can at least modify – eg, talking over people when they are talking or generally being insensitive to another person's feelings.
- **Successful situations.** This is about realising *how* you affect other people. Be aware of the reasons why you were successful and what this tells you about yourself. Was it at the emotional or psychological expense of another person? How could you have achieved the same result in a more sensitive way?
- **Extreme reactions.** If people seem to react to you in extreme ways, the problem is that *you* probably strike them as being extreme. Always assume that it is something that you are doing that is producing reactions in other people. If you do this, you will get nearer to understanding your own behaviour.

In summary, the best advice to someone who wants to 'tone down' his behaviour is to be more aware of the cues about himself that other people give him. Also, he should use this information to adapt the way in which he deals with other people.

3. 'I would like to be more open'

The issue with tough-minded people is that they may lack the ability to project themselves as being genuinely concerned, and they may find it difficult to establish an easy rapport with other people. They can also be very impatient with those who are not performing jobs or doing things in the way in which they would like.

The practical side to being seen as more genuine is to accept that other people, including yourself, are fallible. Also, you should take care to share your thoughts and feelings with those you are dealing with and to make a point of finding out how they feel. These are key aspects of achieving a working rapport with people. In fact, the whole business of establishing rapport has been extensively examined by psychologists. They have found that there are a number of important behaviours:

- **Use of small talk.** This is something the tough-minded person can find irritating (because it appears to waste time), but it is the basis for starting and establishing a relationship. The best approach is to discover some mutually safe topic and to use it to prime the conversation – eg, sports or the news.
- **Being empathic.** Again, the tough-minded person may find that he has little time for other people's problems. But it is an established fact that being able to 'see' problems or situations from another person's perspective is a good way of maintaining rapport. In particular, it is important to demonstrate that you know how it feels and to give other people the space to express their feelings.
- **Use of humour.** This is arguably another behaviour that gets in the way of business, but it is an important tool for putting people at their ease. Telling a joke at your own expense also makes you appear more genuine and human.

Tough-minded people need to accept that there are behaviours that will make them appear more tender minded and thus more approachable. Also, they need to realise that they do not have to be 'tough' with people to achieve results.

4. 'I would like to be less sensitive'

The 'problem' with being tender minded is that you are usually too sensitive to other people and you sometimes feel hurt as a result of what they say or do in their relationship with you. Classic causes of hurt are:

- The feeling that you are being taken for granted.
- A direct criticism of your behaviour.
- An unexpected sarcastic or personal remark.
- Being put down in front of other people.
- Being ignored by someone who knows you well.
- Having your feelings overlooked.

These behaviours can provoke unhappiness, make you feel angry or encourage you to take revenge. It is also the case that these reactions on your part are counterproductive. They do not make you feel better, apart from maybe the revenge option. However, if you really are tender minded, it is unlikely that you will ever put a revenge plan into operation. A better way of dealing with your feelings is to indulge in what psychologists call constructive 'self-talk'. For example:

- 'You really can't please everyone. Some people will always get upset with me.'
- 'Why should I always want people to approve of me? I should be confident in myself.'
- 'This reaction is only revealing a flaw in them. They are obviously rather insecure.'

and, the classic psychiatric mantra:

- 'I decide whether to be hurt or not. It's up to me if I want to be upset.'

As with the tough-minded individual, the other way of changing your behaviour is to adopt an empathic, rather than a sympathetic, style of responding to other people. Empathy concerns 'being with' another person and not losing track of the fact that this is a separate person with his own thoughts and feelings. It is impossible and unrealistic to take on the burden of caring about every single thing that happens to the people you meet. You must realise that it is quite acceptable to put your own emotional welfare first.

5. 'I would like to be more creative'

Those who operate in a conforming way, and so tend to favour rules and regulations, can sometimes benefit from taking a 'looser' view of life. In fact, highly conforming people can learn something from those who are more creative.

Creativity is not necessarily a flash of inspiration, rather it is a process of generating new or improved ideas. It is a reaction against the mindset that states 'that's the way I've always done it', which stands in the way of improving and capitalising on new ideas and techniques.

If you are unfamiliar with creative techniques, they are just ways of 'viewing' a problem from a different angle. An expression that is sometimes used is 'unfreezing' – an appropriate term because it encapsulates the process of moving *away* from fixed and established ways of doing things. The process of unfreezing can also act as the stimulus for what are recognised as the four main creative skills:

- **Fluency.** This is having numerous ideas. The way to do this is to think of every solution you can to a problem. A technique used here is 'brain-storming', which has only two rules: the more ideas, however (apparently) bizarre, the better; and judgement is always left until *after* all the ideas have been generated.
- **Originality.** This is the production of unusual ideas. One method you can use is to avoid logic (lateral thinking). For example, you can simply reverse situations. Imagine that fuel is free at petrol stations, what effect would this have? What would happen if the shop-floor workers decided how much the Managing Director should earn?
- **Flexibility.** This is the production of a range of solutions to a problem. Obviously, you are more likely to

hit on a successful solution if you have more than one thing to choose from. A method that is used here goes under the grand title of 'morphological analysis'. Basically, this involves detailing all the possible combinations of an item. For example, if you were designing a paint container, you could alter the volume, shape and material. In this way you could suggest a one-litre, rectangular, paper container. Well, it works for milk, why not for paint?

■ **Elaboration.** This is the ability to build on existing ideas – an ability that should not be underestimated as many successful products and services are extensions of old ideas. For example, many products or services are based on very old ideas, such as aspects of nature or biological systems.

If you would like to try to use creative techniques, there are many books on the subject. A large bookshop or library will be able to provide you with plenty of choice. However, you should bear in mind that creative techniques, by their very nature, involve an element of risk. So you have to be able to cope with potential failure. However, a quotation by the management guru, Tom Peters, may be useful: 'the way to accelerate your success rate is to double your failure rate'!

6. 'I would like to plan things better'

The highly creative person tends to suffer from a degree of disorganisation. One solution to this problem is to address the question of planning. Paradoxically, while this is viewed by most people as being important, very few actually plan in a logical way. Indeed, the creative person in particular may believe that things are best left to work themselves out and that formal planning stifles their spontaneity. However, in the modern business world it is seldom a good idea to leave things to chance in this way.

Planning is the process of defining a goal and of deciding how you are going to get there. To be effective, the goal must be stated in specific terms and ideally should be measurable, attainable, realistic and time-bounded. This means that you must known that when you have achieved it, it is a realistic target to which you can commit yourself, and that it is underpinned by some sort of timetable. This process, which can be summarised by the mnemonic SMART (Specific, Measurable, Attainable, Realistic, Timebound), forms the basis of informed goal-setting.

In addition to goal-setting, the creative person needs to realise that many business activities, by their very nature, have to be performed in a predictable and methodical way, and that the smallest parts of processes have to be organised and controlled. Thus, while it is valuable to be able to think of new ways of performing tasks, these ideas need to be properly thought out and supported with appropriate evidence. In consequence, if you are in the position of presenting new ideas you should:

- Choose the right time.
- Prepare for likely objections.
- Explain the idea fully and effectively.
- Involve others and (ideally) appeal to their self-interest.
- Generate interest – ie, what are the benefits?
- Justify the use of resources.
- Be enthusiastic!

These are ways of giving your arguments structure and of making them more convincing. In addition, while as the owner of a new idea you may be rightly proud of and want accepted, you should always bear in mind that there is frequently a reaction against anything that upsets the status quo. In the light of this, your best approach is to use your creative drive in a planned and disciplined manner.

7. 'I would like to be less of a perfectionist'

If you are a very high-structure person, you may want to control your desire to organise and control your environment. You may find that your wish *always* to finish jobs to your high personal standards actually hinders your progress, because it is difficult to perform perfectly within specific time deadlines, and that it is almost impossible to live up to your own standards. The reason that you must complete tasks yourself is that you have no external reference point, other than the fact that nobody else seems to do anything as well as you. This can cause real problems if you have a job that involves organising or managing other people. In this situation your perfectionist attitude will make you a very critical person, but more importantly it will make it difficult for you to delegate tasks. Yours will be a 'If you want it done properly, then you've got to do it yourself' approach. Naturally, this will only make matters worse because if you do jobs for people or 'tidy-up' after them, they will never improve. The whole situation can rapidly become completely circular.

The only solution is to step outside your feelings and to accept that not everyone believes that precision is important; that people have different ways of doing things, which may not be the way you would do it, but which can be just as effective. Thus, the crucial thing to explore is how you affect other people. Your ability to plan and to be systematic is no doubt inspirational, but perhaps because of your skills in this area you make other people feel inadequate. You should also consider whether your perfectionism is more of a 'problem' in some situations than in others. Perhaps it would be possible to make a deal with yourself and to give yourself permission to be a perfectionist in some areas if you are not so rigid in others. For example, if you are the sort of person who is very tidy, then try to confine your tidiness to a particular aspect of your life rather than all of it. This could manifest itself in keeping your own office or special room at home tidy and attempting to live with the untidiness in the rest of your world. In fact, while this may sound like a difficult thing to do, it is the only way to start the process of desensitising yourself to other people's clutter. It boils down to altering the way in which you perceive disorder.

8. 'I would like to be more organised'

If you are a low-structure person, you probably have completely the reverse problem of the perfectionist just described. Stereotypically, you are someone who suffers from low personal organisation, who goes through life in a casual and spontaneous way. This can show itself in being absent-minded and, practically, in losing things and being late for appointments.

The answer is to start to plan formally what you need to do. In particular, pay attention to the points made in the previous 'I would like to plan things better' section. Also, because low-structure people frequently have little concept of time – hence they are late for appointments – you could try to manage your time more effectively.

The simplest way to manage your time is to keep a diary. However, there is no point in doing this unless you record the appropriate details and consult it each day. But if you are a low-structure person this probably strikes you as being complete anathema, because you don't like conforming to structured ways of behaving. To complicate matters further, you may also be the sort of person who likes to disregard rules and regulations. So perhaps the only way to square this partic-ular circle is to say that to organise yourself, because it makes you more effective, does not necessarily mean that you have to accept all the restraints that society tries to impose on you.

At a pragmatic level, you will need to:

- Plan ahead.
- Keep proper up-to-date files.
- Delegate to others.

- Cut time 'social grazing' (spending long periods social-ising).
- Control and prioritise paperwork.
- Control procrastination.

You can also use the 'salami' method, which involves breaking jobs down into manageable chunks and deciding what needs to be done first. In particular, you may need to recognise the difference between tasks that are 'important and urgent', 'important and not urgent', 'not important and urgent', and 'not important and not urgent', because while the first sort of task tends to get done, the last two get in the way of the second. It is part of the human condition that unless we discipline ourselves, we spend most of our time dealing with the easiest things, in the latter case the 'not important and not urgent'. In contrast, what you should always do are important things before urgent things.

Overall, the best approach is to get the worst over with first (it will make you feel better), and if you tend to be a procrasti-nator, to tell other people what you are going to do. It is a fact that if you 'go public' you are more likely to get it done. It is also important to realise that you should do difficult tasks during your prime time – ie, the time of day when you work best, which is usually not the first hour, nor the hour before you are ready to go home.

If you embrace some of these ideas you will start to become better organised and to manage your time more effectively.

9. 'I would like to be able to motivate myself'

One of the 'problems' of being a highly confident person is that you can be too placid and easy-going. This may make it diffi-cult for you to motivate yourself and to achieve your full potential. In addition, you may find that you do not react to stressful or difficult situations in the same way as other people. Indeed, you may be what is termed a low-reactive person, and give the impression of being 'thick-skinned' and unresponsive. Sometimes this can work to your disadvantage as you may project, unwittingly, an uncaring or even a smug image.

The solution is to become more aware of other people and to develop a more empathic approach. You also need to consider what would actually move you, and those aspects of work that you find exciting and stimulating. Perhaps the problem is that your confidence is reinforced by a job or a lifestyle that is too easy for you, and which is not providing enough challenge. It may be necessary to re-examine the work or life values that are important to you, and to seek to incorporate more of them in what you do. Some example values were given in the ideal job exercise (achievement, independence, creativity, money, altruism), but it was by no means a complete list, and you could also include the following:

- Excitement. Doing new and stimulating work.
- Status. Having a powerful position.
- Role modelling. Being an inspiration to other people.
- Risk. Gambling for the prospect of money or status.
- Intellectual challenge. Stretching your mind.
- Responsibility. Being in charge of other people.
- Expertise. Being the 'best' in your field.

Some of these may hold the clue to your motivation. If it is a question of wanting to be the best, then further study or a professional course may be the answer. If you desire responsibility, then taking on a more managerial role could be the way ahead. Indeed, being put in charge of other people is a good way to be forced to develop a more open style, and a good arena in which to practise a more consultative and empathic approach. You should also remember that all of these values can be stimulated outside work – eg, by helping in the community or by doing voluntary work. The really important issue is that your rewards are 'self-administered' and that you identify how to motivate yourself. Thus, the ideal situation is to isolate attainable rewards that require considerable effort and a combination of factors to achieve.

10. 'I would like to feel less anxious'

There are many people who would like to be less anxious or emotional, but the first point to realise is that we could not live without anxiety. It is an extremely useful aspect of our personality and behavioural repertoire because it alerts us to 'dangers' and can actually make our minds more agile. However, it is possible to be too emotional and this can be a cause of disorganised thinking, unwanted emotion and even panic. It is also closely related to stress, as being very emotional can cause us to feel stressed.

Like anxiety, stress can either be helpful or make us feel depressed and miserable because there is 'good' stress, or stimulation, and 'bad' stress, or strain. For example, most sales people thrive on the 'kick' (stimulation) they get from selling products to new people every day. Other professionals, such as business executives, suffer strain from being overloaded with too many appointments and having to meet many different people.

The first step to take in controlling feelings of anxiety or stress is to acknowledge those situations in which it is a 'problem'. For example, at work the following are all potential causes of stress:

- Change. Any change to your working environment.
- Selling. Selling products or services, or yourself.
- Time. Having to do things with insufficient time.
- Bureaucracy. Having to fight through many rules and regulations.
- Conflict. Dealing with 'difficult' customers or colleagues.
- Isolation. Having to work by yourself.
- Status. Having no authority or power.
- Promotion. Having poor or badly defined promotion prospects.
- Routine. Having to do boring or undemanding work.
- Support. Having little or no support for what you say or do.

More generally, you may also become anxious in a whole range of non-work situations that involve making decisions or dealing with other people. You may also react in an emotional way to how other people feel. For example, you may become affected by other people's pain or even by the injustice you see in the world.

Whatever the cause, you need to develop ways of coping with those situations that you know make you feel anxious. For instance, you could use strategies such as confrontation or distancing. The first involves getting other people to change their behaviour and so reduce your anxiety; the second is to detach yourself from the situation and forget it. Other important approaches include:

- Goal-setting and time management.
- Being more assertive.
- Relaxation training.

The last suggestion is one of the most important to explore because it provides you with a 'portable' way of reducing anxiety. The important techniques to learn about are muscle relaxation, meditation and visualisation. What is more, you can easily teach yourself about any of these by acquiring one of the many books on the subject. Thus, a visit to a good bookshop or your local library will equip you with a number of extremely practical 'How to ...' publications.

Practising new behaviours

Before we look at the best situations in which you can practise new behaviours, it is worth examining some of the barriers that prevent you from achieving what you want. These barriers are common beliefs that can block change; the two most common are:

- If I have problems I must be inadequate. *Nobody goes through life without encountering problems and without changing the way in which they respond to situations. The process of overcoming obstacles is part of living and has little to do with being inadequate.*

■ It is better to keep your problems to yourself. *Sometimes this is true, but if you want to alter your behaviour successfully, you will need, by definition, to involve other people. The word 'feedback' has been mentioned a number of times in this chapter, and importantly it centres on observing how other people react towards you, and at times actually asking them what they think.*

The point is that in order to change your behaviour, you need to accept that you can improve and that it is a perfectly normal wish to want to project yourself in the best possible light. Indeed, the belief you have in yourself, and the attitudes you have towards people and situations, are some of the few behaviour patterns that are totally within your control.

Some situations are better than others for practising new behaviours. The following guidelines are based on actual research to help people to change their behaviour:

■ If you are going to try out something new, start with situations in which your chances of success are high. For example, if you have a job, do not decide immediately to practise on the boss, but pick a safe situation where you will be able to see immediate benefits from your new behaviour.

■ Choose situations where the other person will not be too surprised. Remember that we expect other people's behaviour to be consistent and are suspicious when somebody suddenly starts to act out of character. Indeed, a common reaction is to think that the person must be guilty of something. Obviously, this attitude is to be avoided at all costs, so make sure that you practise either where others don't know what to expect of you, or in situations where people know you are trying

something new. The latter suggests that you try out
new behaviours with friends, colleagues or partners.

■ All successful change depends on feedback. This
implies that you should practise in situations where
you know quickly what the effect has been. In reality,
this usually means in safe one-to-one situations or
when you are dealing with new contracts or acquaintances.

The Myers-Briggs Type Indicator™

Another way of getting useful and objective feedback is to
complete a personality questionnaire that has been specially
designed for developmental purposes. A good example is the
Myers-Briggs Type Indicator (MBTI®), a questionnaire based
on the work of the Swiss psychologist Carl Jung, which identifies your preferences on four independent dimensions. The
first, extroverted–introverted, should come as no surprise, but
you may be less familiar with the other three.

Extroverted (E)–introverted(I)

Extroverted people have a preference for dealing with the outer
world of people, activities and things. In a work context they
like dealing with other people and seek variety and action. The
introvert, in contrast, is concerned with the inner world of
ideas and information. He or she likes quiet, tends to concentrate on one thing at a time, and prefers to work alone.

Sensing (S)–intuitive (N)

The sensing person focuses on the here-and-now and on information from the senses. He or she uses experience to solve
problems and likes to undertake practical tasks. There is also a
concern with detail and a preference for a step-by-step
approach. Those who are intuitive are concerned with the

future, strategy and possibilities. They like to consider the overview and new ways of doing things.

Thinking (T)–feeling (F)

Thinkers base their decisions on the logical analysis of situations. They tend to be firm minded, critical, no-nonsense sort of people. At times decisions can appear to lack a personal element. In contrast, feeling people use values and subjective information to reach decisions. They enjoy pleasing others and promote an inclusive form of working.

Judging (J)–perceiving (P)

The judging person likes a planned, organised approach to life. He prefers to have things settled and actively seeks structure and schedules. In meetings there may be much talk of purpose and direction, and a laser-like focus on the task in hand. Alternatively, the perceiving individual likes flexibility and spontaneity. The concern is with leaving options open and delaying decisions to allow for last-minute changes.

The results of the questionnaire are used to work out your position on each of the four scales. Your 'type' is then represented by a four-letter code, which is associated with a unique set of behavioural attributes and characteristics. For example, the description for an 'ENTJ' is given below:

Example MBTI® development narrative

ENTJ – Extraverted Intuition with Thinking
People with ENTJ preferences use their Thinking preference to run as much of the world as may be theirs to run. They enjoy executive action and long-range planning. Reliance on Thinking makes them logical, analytical, objectively critical, and not likely to be convinced by anything but reasoning. They tend to focus on ideas, not the people behind the ideas.

They like to think ahead, organise plans, situations and operations related to a project, and make a systematic effort to reach objectives on schedule. They have little patience with confusion or inefficiency, and can be tough when the situation calls for toughness.

They think conduct should be ruled by logic, and govern their behaviour accordingly. They live by a definite set of rules that embody their basic judgements about the world. Any change in their ways requires a deliberate change in their rules.

They are mainly interested in seeing the possibilities beyond the present, obvious, or known. Intuition heightens their intellectual interest, curiosity for new ideas, tolerance for theory, and taste for complex problems.

ENTJs are seldom content in jobs that make no demand upon their Intuition. They are stimulated by problems and are often found in executive jobs where they can find and implement new solutions. Because their interest is in the big picture, they may overlook the importance of certain details. Since ENTJs tend to team up with like-minded people, who may also underestimate the realities of a situation, they usually need a person around with good common sense to bring up overlooked facts and take care of important details.

Like other decisive types, ENTJs run the risk of deciding too quickly, before they have fully examined the situation. They need to stop and listen to the other person's viewpoint, especially with people who are not in a position to talk back. This is seldom easy for them, but if they do not take time to understand, they may judge too quickly, without enough facts or enough regard for what other people think or feel.

ENTJs may need to work at taking Feeling values into account. Relying so much on their logical approach, they may overlook Feeling values – what they care about and what other people care about. If Feeling values are ignored too much, they may build up pressure and find expression in inappropriate ways. Although ENTJs are naturally good at seeing what is illogical and inconsistent, they may need to develop the art of

appreciation. One positive way to exercise their Feeling preference is through appreciation of other people's merits and ideas.
ENTJs who learn to make it a rule to mention what they like,
not merely what needs correcting, find the results worthwhile
both in their work and in their private lives.

MBTI® and Myers-Briggs Type Indicator are registered UK
and US trademarks of Consulting Psychologists Press, Inc.
Oxford Psychologists Press Ltd is the exclusive licensee of
the trademarks in the UK. This extract is reproduced with
permission of the UK licensee.

A full report would also include individual comments on
potential pitfalls and suggestions for development. For an
ENTJ, these might be that you overlook other people's needs,
appear impatient, and that you may suppress your own feelings. The associated suggestions for development would then
be that you should make a point of considering how other
people think and feel, check what is practical before leaping in,
reflect on things before making decisions, and take time to
learn how to identify and value your own feelings.

The insights you can gain from the MBTI are extremely
powerful and can act as an important catalyst to change. In
particular, it gives a focus to the sort of behaviour you need to
practise, and where to practise it.

Places to practise

There are many situations in which you can practise new
behaviours. These include meetings and other business activities, when you buy goods or services, and family or social situations. For example, you could practise being:

- More assertive in meetings.
- More decisive in family situations.
- More aware when somebody comes to you with a problem.
- More proactive in your dealings with sales people.
- More persuasive, more empathic, more organised.

or you could become:

- Less confrontational and combative at work.
- Less sensitive to criticism and 'off-the-cuff' comments.
- Less exacting and perfectionist.
- Less open to stress, less disorganised, less rigid.

The fact is, that if you want to change, all that is required is a little application and some will-power. The benefits can be considerable and can substantially help you to achieve your ambitions at work. However, it should be stressed that all the techniques mentioned in this chapter are ways of changing or coping with particular sorts of existing behaviour. They are *not* ways of permanently changing your personality. Personality, perhaps for very good reasons, is something you have to live with and to nurture.

Key points

- You can change the way you respond to other people.
- You can focus changes by considering your ideal job.
- There are techniques you can use to present yourself positively.
- Wanting to change is perfectly natural – we all do it!

7

The Top UK Personality Questionnaires

A recent survey of psychologists showed that despite the existence of over 30 established personality questionnaires, only three were used to any great extent for selection purposes. These were the Sixteen Personality Factor Questionnaire (16PF™), the Occupational Personality Questionnaire (OPQ®) and, some way behind, the California Psychological Inventory (CPI™). Two others, the Rapid Personality Questionnaire (RPQ) and the Personal Profile Analysis (PPA), also have a considerable following. However, they both tend to be used by personnel specialists rather than by psychologists.

In this chapter the five personality questionnaires are described. We will examine in particular what each one is attempting to measure, what it looks like, and how long it takes to complete.

Sixteen Personality Factor Questionnaire (16PF™)

What is it?

This is one of the top two personality questionnaires and was first used in 1949. It has recently been updated (16PF5) and is probably the most widely used. Like many personality measuring systems, it started life in the USA. As the name implies, it measures 16 aspects of personality.

Who uses it?

It is used by personnel professionals for industrial selection, development and clinical purposes, in many countries across the world. In the UK it is commonly used for selecting graduates, sales, professional and technical staff.

What does it measure?

The 16PF has 16 personality scales:

- Warmth
- Reasoning (general intelligence)
- Emotional stability
- Dominance
- Liveliness
- Rule-consciousness
- Social boldness
- Sensitivity
- Vigilance
- Abstractedness
- Privateness
- Apprehension
- Openness to change
- Self-reliance
- Perfectionism
- Tension

These can be reduced to five main personality scales (The Big Five) or what are called in 16PF speak, 'global factors':

- Extroversion
- Anxiety
- Tough-mindedness
- Independence
- Self-control.

What does it look like?

The questionnaire usually comes in booklet form with a separate answer sheet, but it can also be administered on a personal computer. There are 185 questions to which you answer 'True' or 'False', or if you can't make up your mind, '?', – for example:

I like talking to people at parties   a) True   b) ?   c) False
I'd rather be a farmer than a sales
person   a) True   b) ?   c) False

You should note that, apart from personality, the questionnaire measures reasoning or general intelligence; obviously, there are correct answers to the 15 questions on this scale. Some versions of the questionnaire also allow the psychologist or employer to check for 'motivational distortion' – ie, presenting yourself in an overly favourable light.

How long does it take?

The questionnaire is untimed, but usually takes about 40 minutes to complete.

Occupational Personality Questionnaire (OPQ®)
What is it?

This questionnaire was first published in 1984 and has since become a family of related questionnaires of different designs and lengths. It is one of the few questionnaires written in the UK specifically designed to measure the personality dimensions that relate to work. It is available in 9 different versions and covers 17 languages.

Who uses it?

The OPQ, along with the 16PF, is the questionnaire jostling for number one slot in the UK. It is used very widely for selection and developmental purposes, with many of the 'The Times Top 100' companies using a version of it.

What does it measure?

The longest and most popular version of the questionnaire has 32 personality scales:

- Persuasive
- Controlling
- Independent minded
- Outspoken
- Affiliative
- Socially confident
- Modest
- Democratic
- Caring
- Data rational
- Evaluative
- Behavioural
- Conventional
- Variety seeking
- Adaptable

- Conceptual
- Innovative
- Forward thinking
- Detail conscious
- Rule following
- Relaxed
- Worrying
- Tough minded
- Optimistic
- Trusting
- Emotionally confident
- Vigorous
- Competitive
- Achieving
- Decisive.

The shortest version has six scales:

- Imaginative
- Methodical
- Achieving

- Gregarious
- Emotional
- Sympathetic.

What does it look like?

The questionnaires come as question booklets with separate answer sheets or can be administered using personal or hand-held computers. Most employers use one of two main versions of the questionnaire. The first comprises 104 sets of four statements; out of each set you indicate which one is most like you and which one is least like you. The other version has 230 statements, each one of which you rate on a five-point scale running from 1: 'Strongly Disagree' to 5: 'Strongly Agree'.

Example
Choose which of the four statements is most like you and which the least like you:

I am a person who ...
Enjoys talking to people. ☐
Takes risks. ☐
Often feels upset. ☐
Is competitive. ☐

Plans things well ahead. ☐
Is artistic. ☐
Seeks out other people. ☐
Copes with stress. ☐

Example

	Strongly disagree				Strongly agree
I like talking to strangers.	1	2	3	4	5
I always do what I say I will do.	1	2	3	4	5
I am an inventive person.	1	2	3	4	5
I am always on time for appointments.	1	2	3	4	5

You should note that many of the questionnaires also contain a 'social desirability' scale – ie, statements aimed at finding out whether you are more likely than not to describe yourself in a positive light.

How long does it take?

The questionnaire is untimed, but, depending on the version, takes anywhere between 10 and 60 minutes to complete.

California Psychological Inventory (CPI™)

What is it?

This is a general-purpose personality questionnaire that dates from the 1950s. It has been updated over the years and is now available in two main forms: one has 309 questions (CPI 309), the other 434 (CPI 434). As the name implies, it was developed for use in the USA.

Who uses it?

It is widely used by large organisations to select managers and other staff. It can also be used to test leadership and creative potential, and has applications within organisations for counselling and development purposes.

What does it measure?

The CPI 309 has 14 personality scales:

- Dominance
- Social presence
- Empathy
- Socialisation
- Self-control
- Good impression
- Tolerance

- Achievement (through conformance)
- Achievement (through independence)
- Flexibility
- Creative temperament (or creativity)
- Outgoing
- Organised
- Self-realisation.

CPI 434 measures an additional nine scales:

- Status
- Sociability

- Well-being
- Intellectual efficiency

- Self-acceptance
- Independence
- Responsibility

- Tough mindedness
- Communality (or unusual responses).

What does it look like?

The questionnaire comes as a booklet, which contains either 309 or 434 statements, and has a separate answer sheet. You answer each statement 'True' or 'False'.

Example
I sometimes say things just to
shock other people.   a) True   b) False
I have never lost my temper.   a) True   b) False

The design of the questionnaire and the content of the statements make it difficult to know what aspect of personality is being measured. This is quite legitimate and is designed to stop people 'bending the truth', or putting down what they think is a 'better' answer.

How long does it take?

Both varieties of questionnaire are untimed, but CPI 309 takes about 30 minutes to complete and CPI 434 about 50 minutes.

Rapid Personality Questionnaire (RPQ)

What is it?

The RPQ, a short questionnaire developed at the University of London, was first published in 1990. It is designed to give a rapid and valid assessment of an individual's personality by using an adjective check list. It is available in three versions:

RPQ–1 for development, RPQ–2 for selection, and RPQ–3 for 16–19 year olds.

Who uses it?

RPQ–2 is used by employers to select candidates for a wide range of jobs. It is used in particular in management, sales, technical, financial, clerical and administrative recruitment. RPQ–1 is used for development within organisations, especially for self-awareness training and team building.

What does it measure?

The RPQ has five personality scales:

- Extroversion
- Confidence
- Structure (or personal organisation)
- Tough mindedness
- Conformity.

What does it look like?

The questionnaire comes as a single answer sheet that is scored by computer system. There are 80 adjectives to which you respond on a five-point scale. The scale runs from 1: 'Not like me' to 5: 'Really like me'.

Example

	Not like me			Really like me	
Confident	1	2	3	4	5
Co-operative	1	2	3	4	5
Controlled	1	2	3	4	5
Pushy	1	2	3	4	5
Stable	1	2	3	4	5

How long does it take?

The questionnaire is untimed, but usually takes about 10–15 minutes to complete.

Personal Profile Analysis (PPA)

What is it?

This questionnaire dates back to the 1950s but was only introduced into the UK in 1980. Like the RPQ, it comes in the form of an adjective checklist and is very quick and simple to complete. It is used very widely and is marketed in 35 different countries, being available in 22 different languages.

Who uses it?

The PPA is used for selection and development by many large companies and organisations, in particular those in the food, financial, telecommunications, pharmaceutical and electronic sectors.

What does it measure?

The PPA has four personality scales:

- Dominance
- Influence (sometimes called inducement)
- Submission (sometimes called steadiness)
- Compliance.

These four scales yield information on things such as:

- Drive
- Sensitivity
- Tolerance
- Persuasiveness
- Accuracy
- Involvement
- Commitment
- Diligence.

What does it look like?

The questionnaire comes as a single self-scoring answer sheet. There are 24 sets of four adjectives. For each set you decide which one is most like you and which one is least like you.

Example:

In each row put an 'M' in the box next to the word which is most like you, and an 'L' in the box next to the word which is least like you.

Calm	☐	Hesitant	☐	Playful	☐	Timid	☐
Genuine	☐	Tense	☐	Warm	☐	Perceptive	☐
Hasty	☐	Democratic	☐	Innovative	☐	Private	☐

How long does it take?

The questionnaire is untimed, but usually takes between five and seven minutes to complete.

Note: The PPA is also known and trademarked as the DISC, Performax, PAL or Cleaver. Readers should be aware that in the UK many psychologists have doubts about the effectiveness of the PPA. Indeed, in a recent survey of personality measures conducted for the British Psychological Society, the publishers declined to offer test materials and manuals for review.

8

The Major Test Publishers

The list that follows gives the addresses and telephone numbers of the major UK test publishers. It also gives the names of the personality questionnaires distributed by them. Note that those marked with an asterisk (*) are not usually used for selection.

The questionnaires can only be purchased by appropriately trained psychologists or personnel specialists. The basic training requirements are laid down and monitored by The British Psychological Society. Further training is then usually required to use a particular personality questionnaire.

Unless you are a personnel professional you will not be able to buy or see any of these tests. However, the publishers may be able to send you a catalogue, which will contain some useful background information. It is also valuable to know the names of the questionnaires you could be asked to complete.

Assessment for Selection and Employment
Hanover House
2–4 Sheet Street
Windsor
Berkshire
SL4 1BG
Telephone: 01753 850333
Web site: www.ase-solutions.co.uk

Business Personality Indicator (BPI)
Global Gordon's Personal Profile Inventory (Global GPP–I)
Neo Five Factor Inventory (NEO-FFI)
Sixteen Personality Factory Questionnaire™ (16PF™)

CIM Publications
23 Dunkeld Road
Ecclesall
Sheffield
S11 9JN
Telephone: 0114 2363811

Manchester Personality Questionnaire (MPQ)

The Morrisby Organisation
83 High Street
Hemel Hempstead
Hertfordshire
HP1 3AH
Telephone: 01442 215521
Web site: www.morrisby.co.uk

Objective Personality Tests (OPT)
Personality Research Form (PRF)

Oxford Psychologists Press
Lambourne House
311–321 Banbury Road
Oxford
OX2 7JH
Telephone: 01865 510203

California Psychological Inventory™ (CPI™)
Elements of Awareness – Behaviour, Element B (EAOB)*
Fundamental Interpersonal Relations Orientation –
Behaviour™

(FIRO-B™)*
Myers-Briggs Type Indicator® (MBTI®)*
Note: The MBTI is the most popular questionnaire for staff development.

Psychological Consultancy Ltd
4 Mount Ephraim Road
Tunbridge Wells
Kent
TN1 1EE
Telephone: 01892 547500
Website: www.psyconltd.com

Hogan Development Survey (HDS)
Hogan Personality Inventory (HPI)
Motives, Values, Preferences Inventory (MVPI)

The Psychological Corporation
24–28 Oval Road
London
NW1 7DX
Telephone: 020 7424 4200
Web site: www.psychcorp.com

Orpheus
Giotto

Psytech International Ltd
The Grange
Church Road
Pullox Hill
Bedfordshire
MK45 5HE
Telephone: 01525 720003
Web site: www.psytech.co.uk

Fifteen Factor Questionnaire (15FQ)
Jung Type Indicator (JTI)*
Occupational Personality Profile (OPP)

Saville & Holdsworth Ltd
The Pavilion
1 Atwell Place
Thames Ditton
Surrey
KT7 0NE
Telephone: 0870 070 8000
Web site: www.shlgroup.com

Occupational Personality Questionnaire –
Concept® (OPQ®-C)
Occupational Personality Questionnaire – Factor® (OPQ®-F)
Occupational Personality Questionnaire – IMAGES®

The Test Agency
Cournswood House
North Dean
High Wycombe
Buckinghamshire
HP14 4NW
Telephone: 01494 563384

Rapid Personality Questionnaire (RPQ)

Thomas International Systems Ltd
Harris House
17 West Street
Marlow
Buckinghamshire
SL7 2LS
Telephone: 01628 475366

Personal Profile Analysis (PPA)

Example OPQ32®
Narrative Report

This is an example of a manager's report for the OPQ® questionnaire. As you will see it contains a great deal of detailed information; however, this is just part of a full report. The OPQ® report generation system is capable of producing additional information relating to preferred team roles and leadership style, as well as things like reaction to stress.

The manager's report is designed for the untrained reader and is often the sort of report that will be used in a selection or development situation. As an exercise you might find it interesting to consider a couple of questions while reading Mr Fraser's results:

Do you think that Mr Fraser would make a good manager? If so, what sort of organisation do you think would suit him best?

OPQ32® Expert Report

Manager's Report

Introduction

This report is based upon Mr Fraser's responses to a self-report personality questionnaire, the Occupational Personality Questionnaire (OPQ32i). This questionnaire invited him to describe his behaviour, preferences and attitudes, in relation to different aspects of his working life, by identifying from blocks of four statements, the one that was most, and the one that was least, like him. His responses have been compared against those of a large relevant comparison group to give a profile of Mr Fraser's perceived preferences for different ways of behaving at work. These are grouped into three main areas: Relationships with People, Thinking Style and Feelings, and Emotions.

This report should be treated confidentially. It describes Mr Fraser's personality profile and makes links between various aspects involved. When considering the results of the personality questionnaire, it is important to recognise the responses given were Mr Fraser's own view, and represent the way he sees his behaviour, rather than how his personality might be described by another person. The accuracy of this report depends on the frankness and honesty with which the questionnaire was completed, as well as, in part, on his self-awareness. The comments made here should therefore be seen as tentative rather than infallible. Nevertheless, this self-report can provide important indicators of Mr Fraser's style at work, and it is likely to enable us to predict a good deal about his behaviour in different situations.

Note that the questionnaire describes Mr Fraser's preferred style of behaving rather than his competence or ability. The questionnaire gives a broad picture of his current style, and so the report is necessarily quite general. Greatest values can be gained by discussing the implications of this information against his current or future rule. The shelf-life of the information contained in the report is considered to be 18–24 months, depending on Mr Fraser's work role and personal circumstances. If there have been major changes in his life or there is a significant change in role, he should complete the questionnaire again.

If you have any concerns regarding the content of this report, please raise these with someone who has received full training in the use of OPQ questionnaires.

Relationships with People
Influence

Mr Fraser is likely to have a keen interest in influencing other people for, as well as being extremely interested in selling things to others and entering into negotiation with them, he has a desire to lead people and to take charge of situations. It is likely that managing others, sales and even sales management will appeal to him. Others might find Mr Fraser a challenge to manage because, as well as tending to be prepared to debate and argue his point forcefully, he has a strong tendency to go his own way if others disagree with his point of view. This level of outspokenness and independence may be useful in challenging the prevailing view but could also act as a barrier to reaching consensus. As well as being extremely keen on selling and negotiating, he has a very strong desire to win and to come out on top. A sense of competition is likely to make his desire to 'sell' or persuade even stronger. He is likely therefore to be comfortable within most sales environments where clear targets are set and rewarded.

His attempts to persuade are all the more likely to be successful since he is not frightened to argue his case forcefully and in an outspoken fashion. He may therefore be seen as especially assertive and single-minded when trying to influence others.

He is not afraid to talk about his own achievements and successes and this is likely to gain him credibility when he attempts to persuade or sell to other people.

His strong feeling of confidence and ease with others is likely to strengthen the overall impact that he has when trying to influence. His strong inclination to manage and control the work of others is likely to be driven to a considerable extent by his own agenda, since he has clear views about the way things should be done. This will be further increased by his reluctance to consult with others.

Mr Fraser's management style may be described as autocratic since he has a much stronger tendency to control and manage others than he does to consult and discuss issues with those that he managers. This is likely to result in his being seen as considerably more directive than consultative.

Sociability
He is likely to be very sociable in a number of ways: he tends to be extremely confident when meeting strangers for the first time or addressing a group; and when part of a group he tends to be a lively talker. His preference for spending time in the company of people is very similar to that of most others. In practice, he is likely to feel at ease with people, but also enjoys periods of time alone and will seek out work that offers balance.

In addition to his high profile within a group and very lively nature, he very much enjoys telling others about his successes. This could potentially result in his being seen as quite self-centred and boastful.

Empathy
Mr Fraser describes himself as extremely intolerant of other people's problems and is unlikely to lend much support to others (unless he feels they are in serious trouble), while he tends almost always to make decisions without consulting other people. In addition to this, he is likely to be very vocal about his triumphs and achievements. He may often run the risk of being considered absorbed with himself rather than interested in other people's needs.

Thinking style
Analysis
The main analytical theme for Mr Fraser appears to be people where he reports a strong preference for analysing others' motivations and behaviours. In contrast to this, he reports a disinclination towards working with numerical or statistical information and a similar level of interest to most others in critically analysing information or plans proposed to him. Mr Fraser is therefore most likely to enjoy roles involving understanding people, where quantification of information is kept to a minimum.

His reluctance to work with numerical data is accompanied by a rapid decision-making style, suggesting that his approach could be rather hasty and lacking in a thorough interpretation of statistical trends or data. This instinctive, 'gut feel' approach to making decisions may result in a tendency to take risks, but may also be more typical of highly entrepreneurial individuals.

Creativity and change
Mr Fraser sees himself as intellectually curious, enjoying discussing hypothetical or theoretical issues. When it comes to gathering ideas and challenging existing work methods, however, he is more moderate. He sees himself as only slightly more creative and inventive than his peers, and reports an equal appreciation of new over more established approaches. His reputation is likely to be predominantly one of a theorist who enjoys thinking around a problem without being especially radical or creative.

Mr Fraser reports a level of interest in variety and novelty in his work that is as marked as most of his peers. When he is faced with change or novelty he recognises to a certain extent the need to adapt his behaviour to meet the perceived changing demands of the situations or people. Overall, therefore, his approach to changing situations may be described as fairly typical.

It would appear that, although not strongly averse to

working with established methods and a reasonable amount of routine and repetitive work, he nonetheless does not see deadlines and the completion of ongoing work as a major priority. Although Mr Fraser is intellectually curious and interested in thinking through more abstract concepts, this is not supported by an equal attraction towards analysing numerical or statistical information. This may mean that, whilst his thinking style is likely to be quite sophisticated, it may well be based on more subjective or intuitive analysis than on an in-depth analysis of the facts and data. Although he reports himself as someone who generates a reasonable number of ideas, he is unlikely to subject these to a particularly detailed analysis in order to assess their feasibility. This may be further affected by his tendency to take an optimistic view of the likely success of his own ideas. He may well, therefore, need someone else to take on this more detailed review of his ideas.

Structure

Mr Fraser reports a disinclination for thinking ahead and setting long-term goals, as well as a very clear lack of interest in detail and order. Thus, he seems more concerned with the present than the future and may tend to pay little attention to the more detailed aspects of his work.

Mr Fraser reports only a little less inclination to stick closely to rules and regulations than his peers. On the other hand, he seems to place a lower emphasis upon the importance of meeting deadlines and seeing tasks through to their conclusion.

Mr Fraser's approach when managing others and taking control of situations is likely to be more focused on the immediate than longer term. He may therefore be somewhat more suited to a role where his reports look for instructions on a short-term basis, rather than one requiring a more strategic management style. The strong dislike of detail that he describes is matched by a rather low emphasis on meeting deadlines or completing work on time. It is likely that both of these are at least in part influenced by his moderate need for variety and change in his working day. Mr Fraser's low focus on meeting deadlines and seeing jobs through to the end is likely to be apparent when he is managing and controlling the work of others. He is unlikely to emphasise the importance of these to others when issuing work instructions or providing others with priorities, and this may reduce his effectiveness in some aspects of management control.

Feelings and Emotions
Emotion

Mr Fraser describes himself as relatively free from anxiety or worry. He is likely to find it easy to relax and experiences little tension before important events. He may often be a welcome calming influence on others in tense situations. However, he may also be so relaxed, especially before important occasions, that it could impact upon his motivation or energy levels. Mr Fraser considers himself resilient in the face of criticism, describing himself as unlikely to take offence at insults. Although he has an extremely positive outlook and a resilient nature, he nevertheless tends to feel it is prudent to be suspicious of people. Thus, although his approach may tend to be positive and resilient, he is unlikely to be gullible or easily fooled by others. This combination of characteristics could be useful to someone involved in difficult or protracted negotiations.

He describes himself as someone who keeps his emotions and feelings to himself. He may rarely give an indication to others as to how he feels about things, and may appear uninvolved or unemotional. This may be of benefit when his emotions are particularly negative or unconstructive but not when they might otherwise have communicated enthusiasm. His capacity to brush off insults or criticism is likely to be especially powerful when attempting to sell, or to negotiate with others. This may give him the edge in terms of persisting with a sale, but could cause him to come across as thick-skinned and even insensitive to the feedback that others are trying to give him. His willingness to speak out and criticise others when they disagree with his own strong opinions is consistent with his relative insensitivity to criticism or negative comments. He will be able to shrug off most comments that are passed regarding his perceived stubbornness or inflexibility towards meeting the group consensus. His very positive view is consistent with his reported confidence before important events, as well as his calm and relaxed approach more generally. Overall, this shows him to be a very positive and relaxed individual, although there is the potential danger here that he will be seen as overly optimistic or unconcerned about important activities and events. There is an interesting link between his reported clear interest in managing the work of others, and his perception, however, that they cannot always be trusted. This suggests that others may not find him very empowering, as he is unlikely to express a high degree of confidence in their capabilities and intentions. As well as feeling that others should be viewed with a considerable degree of suspicion, he is likely to make this fairly clearly through his tendency to speak his mind openly.

Dynamism

A major source of drive for Mr Fraser comes from opportunities to compete or compare his performance against that of others, together with a very high level of career ambition. Together these are likely to cause him to focus upon his career success and how he compares with his peers or other reference group. Further, he enjoys keeping fairly busy at work and this is likely to provide him with the energy to achieve a number of these ambitions. He reaches decisions quickly. This is likely to be received well in an environment where risk-taking is acceptable, but less desired in a situation where mistakes can lead to very serious consequences, perhaps financial, or where people's safety is at risk.

As well as describing himself as a very competitive person, he also enjoys roles that offer him the opportunity to sell or to persuade others. Together these suggest someone who may well thrive within a traditional salesperson role, motivated by competitive targets and feedback regarding his own performance against that of his colleagues in a similar role.

His highly competitive nature is perhaps consistent with his desire to remain very detached from others' personal problems. Together these suggest someone who is predominantly concerned with his own performance in comparison with that of others' and he could come across as more focused on himself than others. Indeed, this is further supported by his ability to brush off any negative comments or feedback that he may receive as a result of his behaviour.

His very strong need to win in competitive situations is unlikely to be very noticeable to those around him as he tends to keep his feelings hidden. Those with whom he is competing may therefore be rather surprised at how important winning is to him.

His considerable level of career ambition appears to include an interest in managing and leading others. He may well, therefore, be motivated by opportunities to progress his career in this direction. In addition, he is likely to set others high goals and targets as part of his management role. When thinking about his career progression and the targets that he sets himself, he is unlikely to take a particularly forward-thinking, or long-term perspective. This could mean a more reactive, or generalised, sense of where he wishes to get to, or perhaps a greater focus on the short-term in relation to his career goals.

As well as making fast decisions, his strong tendency to be optimistic and have a positive expectation of future events may mean that they are based upon his rather rosy view of the likely outcome of his decisions.

Further Information

There are many books on psychological testing, psychometrics and personality. Many of them are very technical and difficult to understand, but if you are seriously interested in the psychology of personality, the mechanics of personality testing or just how tests work, the following may be of interest:

The Essentials of Psychological Testing by Lee Cronbach. Published by Harper & Row, 1984. This is the classic student text on psychological testing.

The Handbook of Psychological Testing by Paul Kline. Published by Routledge, 1994. A professional handbook for those who want to design their own tests.

The Organisation Man by William Whyte. Published by Simon & Schuster, 1956. Famously, it contains advice on 'How to cheat at Personality Tests'.

Personality at Work by Adrian Furnham. Published by Routledge, 1994. The role of personality testing in the management of the workplace.

Personality: The psychometric view by Paul Kline. Published by Routledge, 1993. A good modern review of personality testing and questionnaires.

Psychological Testing by Anne Anastasi. Published by Macmillan, 1982. A comprehensive book that covers all aspects of psychological testing and test construction.

Psychological Testing: A manager's guide by John Toplis, Victor Dulewicz and Clive Fletcher. Published by the Institute of Personnel & Development, 1987. A good general guide for managers, it considers the use of psychological tests.

Review of Personality Assessment Instruments (Level B) for Use in Occupational Settings by David Bartram *et al.* Published by The British Psychological Society, 1995. The best source of information on all the major UK personality questionnaires.

Using Psychology in Business by Mark Parkinson. Published by Gower, 1999. This is the latest book on how psychological techniques can be used to grow businesses.

Using Psychometrics by Robert Edenborough. Published by Kogan Page, 1994. The most up-to-date and understandable guide for managers interested in testing.

If you want to try other sorts of psychological tests and questionnaires, Kogan Page publishes a comprehensive range of books containing example questions.

Epilogue

'Life is what happens to you when you are busy
making other plans.'

John Lennon

In this book I have taken you on a journey of discovery. I have
asked you to think about what personality is and how it is
assessed. I have also tried to make you think about yourself, to
interpret your own personality and to consider what you find.
In many ways this is an unusual thing to do because most of us
never consider our personalities in an objective manner.
However, it is only when we understand ourselves and how
others see us that we can change.

The process of change does not involve altering your basic
personality, but rather focusing it, and adding different sorts of
behaviour to your natural repertoire. It is rather like acting
because it involves projecting yourself as you would like others
to see you. Unlike acting, however, it involves altering your
image in a real arena, that of work or of personal relationships.

Ultimately, the secret of success with any form of personality
assessment is to know yourself and, with that knowledge, to
present yourself in the most positive way you can. I hope
this book will help you to do this. Good luck with all your
endeavours.

Further Reading from Kogan Page

Career, Aptitude and Selection Tests, Jim Barrett, 1998

Great Answers to Tough Interview Questions, 4th edition, Martin John Yate, 1998

How to Master Psychometric Tests, 2nd edition, Mark Parkinson, 2000

How to Pass Computer Selection Tests, Sanjay Modha, 1994

How to Pass Graduate Recruitment Tests, Mike Bryon, 1994

How to Pass Numeracy Tests, 2nd edition, Harry Tolley and Ken Thomas, 2000

How to Pass Selection Tests, 2nd edition, Mike Bryon and Sanjay Modha, 1998

How to Pass Technical Selection Tests, Mike Bryon and Sanjay Modha, 1993

How to Pass the Civil Service Qualifying Tests, Mike Bryon, 1995

How You Can Get That Job!, 2nd edition, Rebecca Corfield, 1999

Interviews Made Easy, 2nd edition, Mark Parkinson, 1998

The Job Hunter's Handbook, 2nd edition, David Greenwood, 1999

Job Hunting Made Easy, 3rd edition, John Bramham and David Cox, 1995

Preparing Your Own CV, 2nd edition, Rebecca Corfield, 1999

Readymade CVs, 2nd edition, Lynn Williams, 2000

Readymade Job Search Letters, 2nd edition, Lynn Williams, 2000

Test Your Own Aptitude, 2nd edition, Jim Barrett and Geoff Williams, 1990